PEOPLE, PLANET AND PURPOSE

INTERDISCIPLINARY INSIGHTS FOR THE 21ST CENTURY

Editors

Dr Geetika Singh

Dr. Mohd.Farman Ali

SAMANT PUBLISHING

ISBN : 9788199862524

Edition : First, March 2026

Title : People, Planet and Purpose- Interdisciplinary insights for the 21st century

Editors : Dr Geetika Singh, Dr. Mohd.Farman Ali

Published by

SAMANT PUBLISHING

An Imprint of **Taneesha and Prachi NextGen Publication**

Registered Address: Plot No. 48, Khasra No. 646, Road No. 2,
Suman Nagar, Bahadarabad, Haridwar, Uttarakhand – 249402, India
Website : www.samantpublishing.com
E-mail : support@samantpublishing.com
Phone : +91 9760418103

Printed by :
Manipal Technologies Limited, Bengaluru - 560001, Karnataka

Acknowledgment

The authors express their sincere gratitude to all those who have supported and encouraged us in the completion of this book, ***People, Planet and Purpose***.

We are deeply thankful to the management and administration of Madhav University for providing a supportive academic environment that encourages research, learning, and intellectual growth. We would especially like to acknowledge ***our Respected Chairman Sir Dr Rajkumar Rana*** for its continuous encouragement and cooperation throughout the development of this work.

Our heartfelt appreciation goes to our colleagues and students whose discussions, insights, and curiosity inspired many of the ideas presented in this book. Their enthusiasm for learning and commitment to understanding contemporary global challenges motivated us to explore the themes of people, sustainability, and purpose more deeply.

We are also grateful to our families and well-wishers for their constant encouragement, patience, and unwavering support during the writing process.

Finally, we extend our sincere thanks to all readers. We hope that this book contributes meaningfully to the understanding of sustainable development and inspires thoughtful action toward a better future.

By:

Respected Authors

Madhav University

Preface

People, Planet and Purpose – Interdisciplinary Insights for the 21st Century

The twenty-first century confronts humanity with a paradox. Never before have we possessed such extraordinary technological capability, scientific understanding, and global connectivity. And yet, never before have we faced challenges of such complexity—climate disruption, widening inequality, social fragmentation, public health crises, ecological degradation, and rapid technological transformation. These are not isolated problems. They are interconnected realities, woven tightly together across borders, cultures, and disciplines.

People, Planet and Purpose was born from a simple but urgent conviction: the challenges of our time cannot be solved in silos.

For generations, knowledge has been organized into disciplines—economics separated from ecology, technology from ethics, policy from philosophy, and science from the humanities. This structure has allowed depth and specialization. But the crises we face today demand integration. The well-being of people is inseparable from the health of the planet. Economic systems are intertwined with ecological systems. Innovation without ethical direction risks deepening inequality. Sustainability without social justice cannot endure. Progress without purpose becomes perilous.

This book invites readers to explore the intersections.

At its heart are three foundational pillars:

People – Human dignity, equity, health, culture, and community. How do we design systems that empower rather than marginalize? How can education, governance, and technology uplift humanity instead of divide it? Planet – Ecological resilience, biodiversity, climate stability, and sustainable resource use. What does stewardship mean in an era of planetary boundaries? How do we reconcile growth with regeneration?

Purpose – Meaning, values, ethics, and long-term vision. Why do we innovate? For whom? Toward what future? Purpose connects policy with morality, enterprise with responsibility, and knowledge with wisdom.

Throughout these pages, scholars and practitioners from diverse fields—environmental science, economics, public policy, sociology, engineering, philosophy, and beyond—contribute insights that illuminate both tensions and possibilities. Some chapters analyze systemic risks; others propose transformative frameworks. Some explore emerging technologies; others examine indigenous knowledge systems and ancient philosophies. Together, they offer not a single solution, but a mosaic of perspectives.

Inter disciplinarity is not merely an academic method—it is a way of thinking. It asks us to listen across boundaries, to embrace complexity rather than reduce it, and to recognize that sustainable futures are co-created. It challenges reductionism and calls for systems thinking. It encourages humility in the face of uncertainty and courage in the face of change.

The concept of "purpose" threads the narrative together. In a world driven by metrics of efficiency and profit, purpose reminds us of values. It urges institutions to align strategy with stewardship, innovation with inclusion, and leadership with accountability. Purpose transforms sustainability from a compliance requirement into a moral commitment.

This preface is not a promise of easy answers. The issues discussed here are multifaceted and evolving. Instead, it is an invitation—to reflect, to question assumptions, to integrate knowledge, and to act with intention.

If this book succeeds, it will not only inform but inspire. It will encourage educators to rethink curricula, policymakers to adopt systems approaches, business leaders to integrate sustainability into core strategy, technologists to embed ethics in design, and citizens to see themselves as participants in shaping a shared future.

The 21st century will be defined not solely by technological advancement, but by our collective capacity to harmonize people, planet, and purpose. The path ahead demands imagination anchored in responsibility, innovation guided by values, and collaboration grounded in empathy.

May these pages serve as a catalyst—for dialogue, for discovery, and for decisive action.

The future is not something we inherit. It is something we create—together.

Index

Chapter 1

Science, Society and Interdisciplinary Thinking

Abhilasha Roy
M.Sc. Research Scholar, College of Agriculture, Madhav University, Pindwara, Sirohi (Raj)

Dr. Neha Tomar
Block Technology Manager (ATMA), Block Pansemal, Dist. Barwani, M.P.

Science, society and interdisciplinary thinking are closely interconnected aspects of human development. Science provides systematic knowledge about the natural and physical world. Society shapes how that knowledge is produced and used. Interdisciplinary thinking ensures that complex problems are approached from multiple perspectives. In the modern era, where global challenges are increasingly interconnected, understanding the relationship between these three elements is essential for sustainable progress and responsible innovation.

1. Science

Science is a systematic way of understanding the natural world through observation, experimentation and evidence-based reasoning. It helps us develop technologies, improve health, protect the environment and expand knowledge. However, science does not operate in isolation—it is shaped by social values, funding priorities, culture and political decisions.

2. Society

Society includes communities, institutions, governments and cultural systems that influence how people live and interact. Society determines which scientific research is supported, how discoveries are used and what ethical limits are placed on innovation. For example, public opinion and laws guide how new medical treatments or artificial intelligence systems are developed and applied.

3. Interdisciplinary Thinking

Interdisciplinary thinking means combining knowledge and methods from different subjects—such as biology, economics, sociology, engineering and ethics—to address issues that cannot be solved by one field alone. Modern challenges like climate change, pandemics, cyber security and sustainable development require cooperation across multiple disciplines.

Science as a Dynamic Process

Science is not merely a body of facts; it is an organized method of inquiry. It relies on observation, experimentation, evidence and critical reasoning to generate explanations about natural phenomena. One of the defining features of science is that it is self-correcting. Theories and explanations are continuously tested and refined as new evidence emerges.

Scientific advancements have dramatically transformed human life. Developments in medicine have reduced mortality rates and increased life expectancy. Innovations in engineering and technology have revolutionized communication, transportation and industry. Environmental science has expanded our understanding of ecosystems and climate systems, allowing for better conservation and sustainability practices.

However, science does not develop in isolation. Research priorities are influenced by social needs, economic investments and political decisions. For example, global health emergencies often lead to increased funding for medical research. Similarly, environmental concerns encourage scientific investigation into renewable energy and sustainable technologies. Thus, science both influences society and responds to it.

Society's Role in Shaping Science

Society plays a critical role in guiding scientific development. Cultural values, ethical standards, public opinion and government policies all shape the direction and application of research. Scientific discoveries may offer new possibilities but society determines how and whether those possibilities are implemented.

Advances in biotechnology, artificial intelligence and data science raise important moral questions. For instance, genetic modification can help eliminate hereditary diseases but it also raises concerns about inequality and unintended consequences. Artificial intelligence can increase efficiency in various sectors, yet it prompts debates about privacy, employment and decision-making authority.

Regulation and governance are also societal mechanisms that influence science. Laws ensure that research involving human participants, animals or environmental risks meets ethical standards. Public engagement in science policy strengthens democratic decision-making and promotes transparency.

Moreover, education strengthens the relationship between science and society. Scientific literacy enables individuals to evaluate evidence, make informed decisions and participate meaningfully in civic discussions. A society that values scientific understanding is better prepared to address misinformation and global challenges.

The Importance of Interdisciplinary Thinking

While scientific disciplines have traditionally developed as specialized fields, many contemporary issues cannot be effectively addressed by one discipline alone. Interdisciplinary thinking involves integrating knowledge, methods and perspectives from different academic and professional areas to solve complex problems.

For example, climate change involves atmospheric science, economics, sociology, political science and engineering. Addressing it requires technological innovation, policy reforms, behavioral change and international cooperation. Similarly, public health crises require collaboration among medical researchers, statisticians, communication experts, psychologists, and policymakers.

Interdisciplinary approaches encourage innovation by fostering collaboration. When experts from different backgrounds work together, they can combine insights in ways that lead to creative and effective solutions. The integration of biology and computer science, for instance, has created bioinformatics, which plays a crucial role in genetic research and personalized medicine. Likewise, the merging of engineering and healthcare has advanced medical device development.

Interdisciplinary thinking also helps ensure that solutions are socially responsible. A purely technical solution may fail if it ignores cultural practices or economic realities. By considering multiple dimensions—scientific, social, ethical, and economic—interdisciplinary approaches produce more balanced outcomes.

The Interconnected Relationship

Science generates knowledge and innovation. Society provides the context, support and ethical boundaries within which science operates. Interdisciplinary thinking connects diverse forms of expertise to address multifaceted problems. Together, these elements form a continuous cycle of development and reflection.

In today's globalized world, challenges such as pandemics, cyber security threats, food insecurity and environmental degradation cross national and disciplinary boundaries. Solutions require collaboration not only among scientists but also among governments, communities and international organizations. Interdisciplinary cooperation strengthens the ability to respond effectively and sustainably.

Furthermore, this integrated approach promotes responsible innovation. Scientific progress should align with societal values and long-term well-being. When science, society and interdisciplinary thinking work together, they support ethical decision-making, inclusive development and global sustainability.

Conclusion

Science, society, and interdisciplinary thinking are deeply interdependent. Science expands knowledge and creates new possibilities. Society shapes how scientific knowledge is developed, regulated and applied. Interdisciplinary thinking bridges specialized fields to address complex and interconnected challenges.

As global issues become increasingly complicated, collaboration across disciplines and awareness of social implications become essential. By fostering scientific literacy, ethical responsibility and interdisciplinary cooperation, societies can ensure that scientific advancements contribute positively to human welfare and sustainable development.

I Answer the Multiple Choice Questions

1. What is the primary goal of interdisciplinary thinking?

A. To separate subjects for deeper specialization

B. To combine knowledge from multiple disciplines to solve complex problems

C. To focus only on scientific methods

D. To replace traditional subjects

2. How does science contribute to society?

A. By creating only laboratory-based knowledge

B. By developing technologies and solutions that improve quality of life

C. By avoiding social issues

D. By limiting innovation

3. Which of the following is an example of interdisciplinary work?

A. A physicist studying motion

B. A chemist analyzing compounds

C. A team of doctors, engineers, and data scientists developing medical devices

D. A historian writing about ancient civilizations

4. Why is ethical consideration important in scientific research?

A. To slow down discoveries

B. To increase competition

C. To ensure research benefits society without causing harm

D. To reduce funding

5. Which issue requires an interdisciplinary approach?

A. Solving a simple arithmetic equation

B. Understanding climate change

C. Memorizing a definition

D. Learning a single formula

6. What role does society play in scientific development?

A. Society has no influence on science

B. Society funds, regulates, and benefits from scientific progress

C. Society stops scientific progress

D. Society replaces scientists

7. Interdisciplinary thinking encourages students to:

A. Ignore other subjects

B. Think critically and connect ideas across fields

C. Avoid teamwork

D. Memorize facts without understanding

8. Technology is best described as:

A. Theoretical knowledge without application

B. The practical application of scientific knowledge

C. A replacement for science

D. A social theory

9. Collaboration between scientists and policymakers helps to:

A. Reduce scientific accuracy

B. Make informed decisions for public welfare

C. Stop innovation

D. Eliminate public opinion

10. Which skill is most important for interdisciplinary problem-solving?

A. Rote memorization

B. Isolation from others

C. Communication and cooperation

D. Avoiding new ideas

II Give the answer of these questions in a descriptive manner

1. Explain the relationship between science and society. How do they influence each other in everyday life?

2. Discuss the importance of interdisciplinary thinking in solving modern global challenges.

3. How does scientific advancement contribute to social development? Provide relevant examples.

4. Examine the role of ethics in scientific research and innovation. Why is it essential?

5. Describe how collaboration between different fields of study leads to effective problem-solving.

6. Analyze the impact of technology on society. Mention both positive and negative effects.

7. Why is critical thinking important in interdisciplinary studies? Explain with suitable illustrations.

8. Discuss how education systems can promote interdisciplinary learning among students.

9. Explain how public policies are influenced by scientific research. Give examples to support your answer.

10. Evaluate the role of communication and teamwork in advancing scientific knowledge and benefiting society.

Chapter 2

Plant Science and Its Role in Sustainable Ecosystems Plant Science and Its Role in Sustainable Ecosystems

Dr Geetika Singh
Assistant professor, dept of basic and applied sciences,
madhav university sirohi

1. Introduction to Plant Science

Plant science, also known as **botany**, is the scientific study of plants, including their structure, growth, reproduction, metabolism, and interactions with the environment. Plants form the **foundation of life on Earth** by producing food, oxygen, and raw materials essential for the survival of all living organisms. Understanding plant science is crucial for addressing modern challenges such as **climate change, food security, biodiversity loss, and environmental sustainability**.

A sustainable eco system is one that maintains ecological balance while supporting life over long periods. Plant science plays a central role in building and maintaining such ecosystems by explaining how plants grow, interact with other organisms, and respond to environmental changes.

Plant science is the study of plants and their vital role sin sustaining life on Earth. From the food we eat and the air we breathe to the materials we use for shelter, clothing, and medicine, plants form the foundation of human survival and environmental stability. Understanding plants—their structure, growth, reproduction, and interactions with the environment—is essential for addressing global challenges such as food security, climate change, and biodiversity loss.

This chapter introduces the basic concepts of plant science, also known as botany. It explores the diversity of plants, ranging from simple mosses to complex flowering plants, and highlights the unique characteristics that distinguish plants from other living organisms. Key topics include plant cells and tissues, photosynthesis, plant nutrition, growth, and reproduction. The chapter also emphasizes the importance of plants in ecosystems, agriculture, and industry.

By studying plant science, students gain insight in to how plants function, adapt, and contribute to life on Earth. This foundational knowledge provides a basis for further study in agriculture, environmental science, biotechnology, and related fields, while fosteringan appreciation for the essential role plants play in maintaining a balanced and sustainable world.

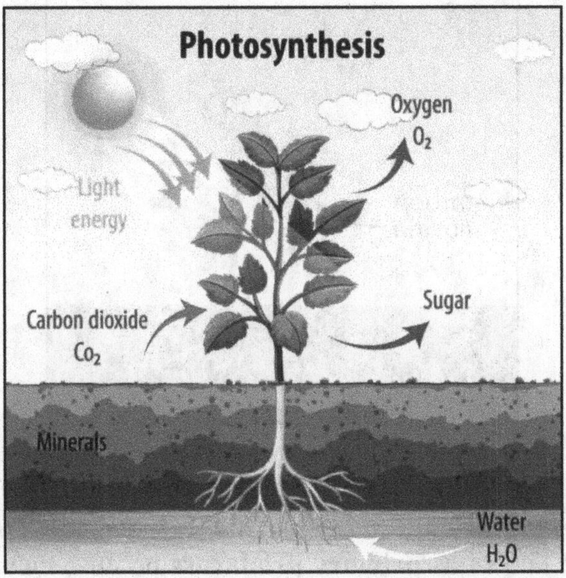

Fig 1: Diagram showing Photosynthesis with intake of carbon dioxide and water showing release of oxygen and sugar

2. Plants as Primary Producers in Ecosystems

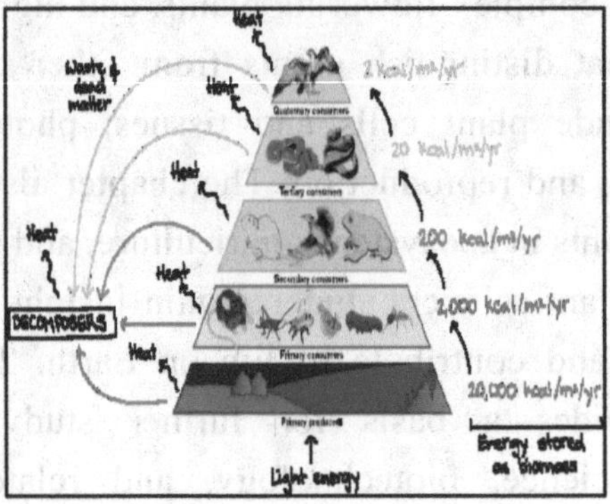

Fig2: Diagram showing Pyramid of Plant as producers in ecosystem

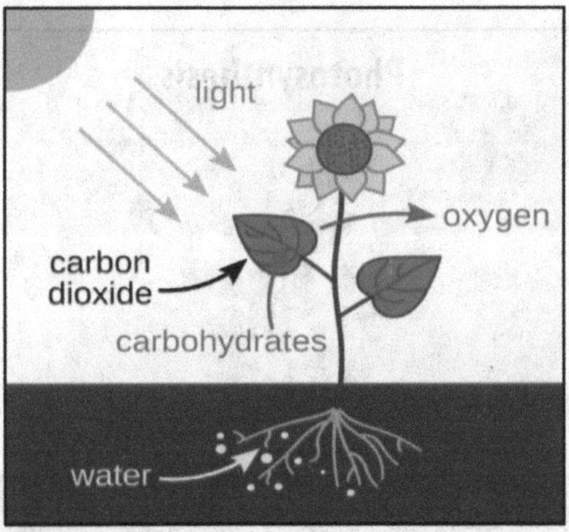

Fig3: Plants showing as primary producers in the presence of sunlight

Plants are known as **primary producers** because they are capable of synthesizing their own food through the process of **photosynthesis**. Using sunlight, carbon dioxide, and water, plants produce glucose and release oxygen as a by-product.

Plants play a fundamental role in ecosystems as primary producers, forming the base of nearly all food chains on Earth. Primary producers are organisms capable of synthesizing their own food from inorganic substances, and plants achieve this through the process of photosynthesis. By converting solar energy into chemical energy, plants support not only their own growth and survival butals the existence of all other living organisms, directly or indirectly. Without plants and other photosynthetic organisms, life as we know it would not be possible.

Atthecoreofplants'roleasprimaryproducersisphotosynthesis.Usings unlight, carbon dioxide from the atmosphere, and water absorbed through their roots, green plants manufacture glucose and other carbohydrates. Chlorophyll, the green pigment found in chloroplasts, captures light energy and drives this process. Oxygen is released as a by-product, making plants the primary source of atmospheric oxygen. This oxygen is essential for respiration in most living organisms, highlighting the central role of plants in maintaining life-supporting conditions on Earth.

As primary producers, plants form the first trophic level in ecosystems. The energy stored in plant tissues becomes available to other organisms when plants are consumed by herbivores. These herbivores, in turn, are eaten by carnivores and omnivores, transferring energy through successive trophic levels. Although energy is lost at each step in the form of heat due to metabolic activities, the initial energy captured by plants sustains the entire food web. Thus, the productivity and health of plant communities directly influence the abundance and diversity of organisms at higher trophic levels.

Plants also contribute significantly to ecosystem structure and stability. Interrestrial ecosystems, vegetation determines habitat availability and physical conditions. Forests, grasslands, and deserts are defined largely by the dominant plant types present. Trees provide shade, regulate temperature, and create microclimates that allow many other organisms to thrive. Grasslands support large populations of grazing animals, while shrubs and groundcover plants prevent soil erosion and maintain soil fertility. In aquatic ecosystems, phytoplankton—microscopic photosynthetic plants—serve as the primary producers, forming the foundation of marine and freshwater food webs. Another critical role of plants as primary producers is their involvement in nutrient cycling. Plants absorb essential nutrients such as nitrogen, phosphorus, potassium, and trace elements from the soil or water. These nutrients are incorporated into plant tissues and later transferred to consumers through feeding. When plants and animals die, decomposers break down their remains, returning nutrients to the environment where they can be reused by plants. In this way, plants act as a vital link between the physical environment and living organisms, ensuring the continuous movement of nutrients within ecosystems.

Plants also play a major role in regulating the global carbon cycle. Through photosynthesis, plants remove carbon dioxide from the atmosphere and store it in organic compounds. Large amounts of carbon are stored in forests, grasslands, and soils, helping to moderate atmospheric carbon dioxide levels and reduce the impact of climate change. When plants respire, decay, or are burned, carbon is released back into the atmosphere, but healthy, growing plant populations help maintain a balance. Deforestation and land degradation disrupt this balance, emphasizing the importance of conserving plant ecosystems.

In addition to their ecological roles, plants as primary producers have immense economic and cultural significance. Agriculture depends entirely on plants to produce food, fiber, fuel, and raw materials for countless industries. Crops such as rice, wheat, maize, and legumes form the dietary foundation for much of the world's population. Natural ecosystems also provide ecosystem services—such as pollination, water regulation, and soil formation—that are ultimately roote din plant productivity. Many cultures have deep spiritual and traditional connections to plants, recognizing their life-giving importance. Environmental changes and human activities increasingly threaten plants and their ability to function as primary producers. Climate change, pollution, deforestation, and habitat destruction reduce plant diversity and productivity, weakening ecosystem resilience. Loss of primary producers can lead to ecosystem collapse, as energy flow and nutrient cycling are disrupted. Protecting plant diversity and promoting sustainable and-use practices are the re foreessential for maintaining healthy eco systems and ensuring long-term survival of life on Earth.

In conclusion, plants are indispensable primary producers in ecosystems. Through photosynthesis, they capture solar energy, produce food and oxygen, and support all other forms of life. Their roles in energy flow, nutrient cycling, habitat formation, and climate regulation make them central to ecosystem function and stability.

2.1. Role in Energy Flow

All food chains and food webs begin with plants. Herbivores depend directly on plants for food, while carnivores depend indirectly on plants through herbivores. Thus, plants are the **base of energy flow** in ecosystems.

2.2. Oxygen Production

Photosynthesis releases oxygen into the atmosphere, making aerobic life possible. Forests, grasslands, and aquatic plants collectively maintain atmospheric oxygen levels, supporting both terrestrial and aquatic life.

3. Plant Science and Nutrient Cycling

Plants play a key role in **bio geo chemical cycles**, which recycle nutrients essential for life.

3.1. Carbon Cycle

Plants absorb carbon dioxide from the atmosphere and store carbon in their tissues. Forests and grass lands act as **carbon sinks**, reducing greenhouse gases and mitigating climate change.

3.2. Nitrogen Cycle

Certain plants, especially legumes, form symbiotic relationships with nitrogen-fixing bacteria. These bacteria convert atmospheric nitrogen into forms usable by plants, enriching soil fertility naturally.

3.3. Soil Health and Decomposition

When plants shed leaves or die, decomposers break down plant material, returning nutrients to the soil. Healthy plant cover prevents soil erosion and maintains soil structure.

4. Role of Plant sin Biodiversity Conservation

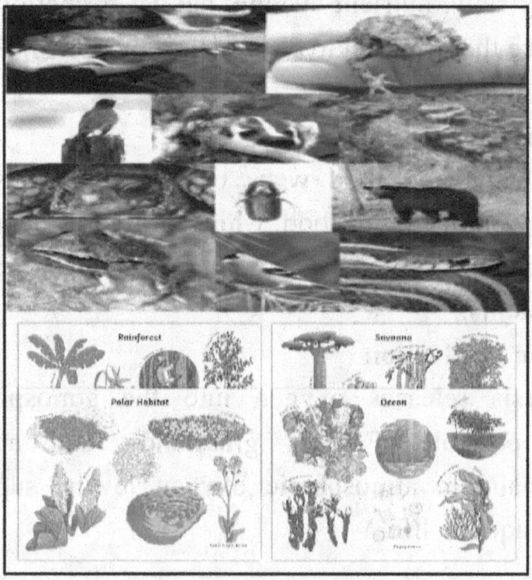

Fig: Role of Plant sin conservation of biodiversity

Fig: Plant diversity supports eco system stability and resilience.

4.1. Habitat Formation

Plants provide food, shelter, and breeding sites for countless organisms. Trees host birds and insects, grasses support herbivores, and a quatic plants shelter fish and amphibians.

4.2. Key stone and Native Species

Some plants, called **keystone species**, have a disproportionately large impact on ecosystems. Native plants are especially import ant because local organisms are adapted to them. Plant science helps identify and protect such species.

5. Plant Adaptations and Ecosystem Stability

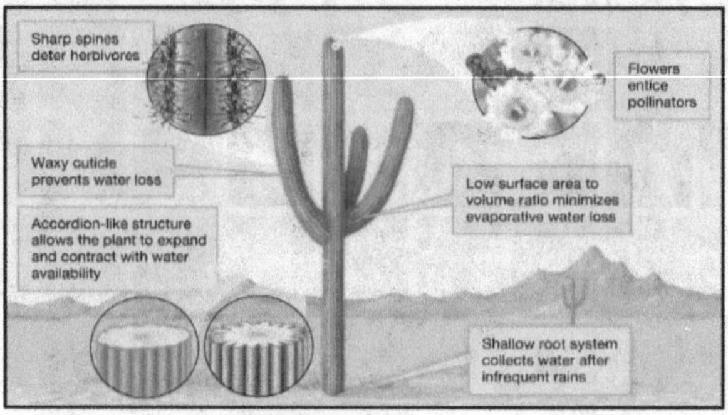

Fig: Stability of Ecosystem with plants showing adaptation

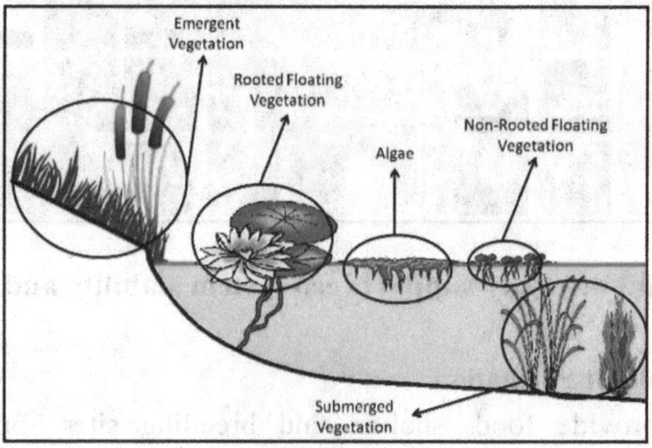

Fig: Different types of vegetation

Plants have evolved a wide range of adaptations to survive indifferent environments.

5.1. Structural Adaptations

- Thick cuticles and spines in desert plants reduce water loss.
- Broad leaves in tropical plants maximize light absorption.

5.2. Physiological Adaptations

Some plants use specialized photosynthetic pathways (C_4andCAM) to conserve water and increase efficiency in extreme climates.

These adaptations help eco systems remain functional under changing environmental conditions.

6. Plant Science in Sustainable Agriculture

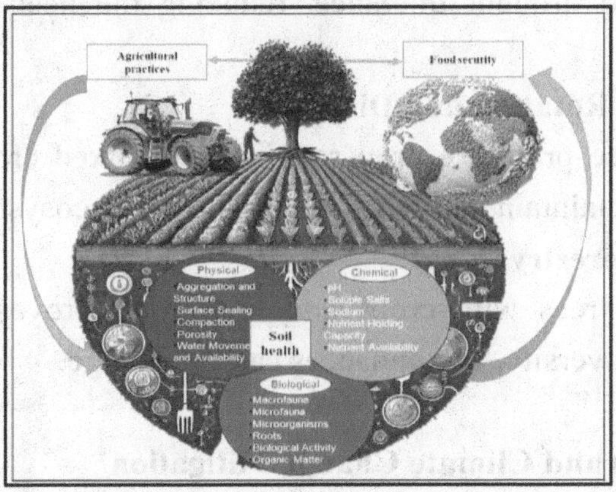

Fig: Cycle showing food security and agricultural practices

Fig: Diagram showing sustainable agriculture

One of the most practical applications of plant science is in **sustainable agriculture**, which aims to produce food while conserving natural resources.

6.1. Crop Improvement

Plant breeding and bio technology improve crop yield, disease resistance, and drought tolerance, reducing the need for chemical inputs.

6.2. Crop Rotation and Diversity

Plant science promotes crop rotation and mixed cropping, which reduce pests, maintain soil fertility, and increase ecosystem stability.

6.3. Agroforestry

Integrating trees with crops and lives to improves soil quality, increases biodiversity, and enhances carbon storage.

7. Plants and Climate Change Mitigation

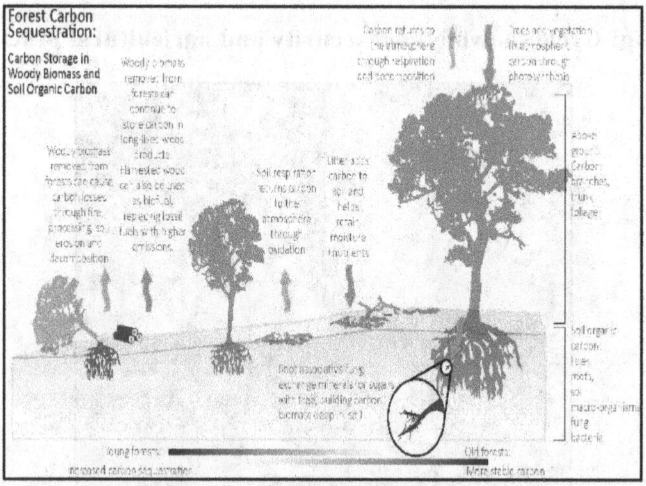

Fig: Plants showing climate change mitigation

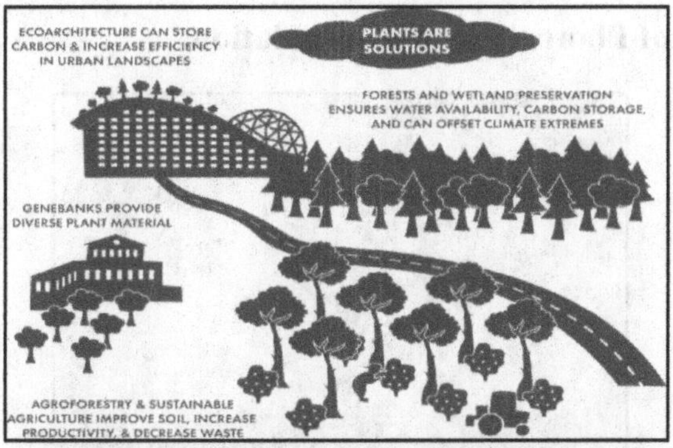

Fig: Plant science is essential in addressing climate change.

7.1. Carbon Sequestration

Forests, mangroves, and grass lands absorb and store large amounts of carbon dioxide. Reforestation and afforestation are effective strategies for climate mitigation.

7.2. Urban Green Spaces

Plants in cities reduce heat, improve air quality, and enhance human well-being. Urban forestry is increasingly important in sustainable city planning.

8. Role of Plants in Water Regulation

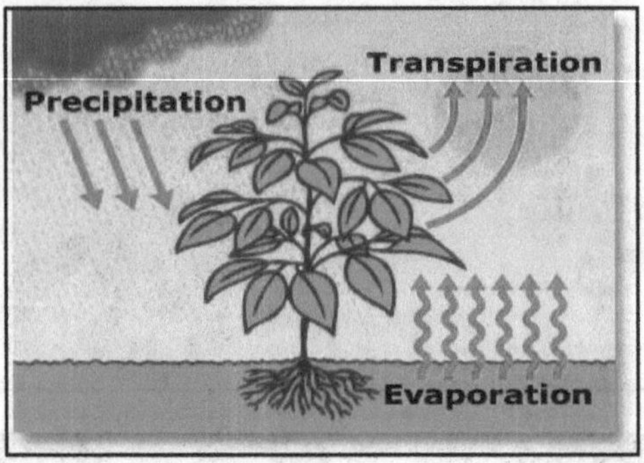

Fig: Diagram showing evaporation and regulation of water in plants

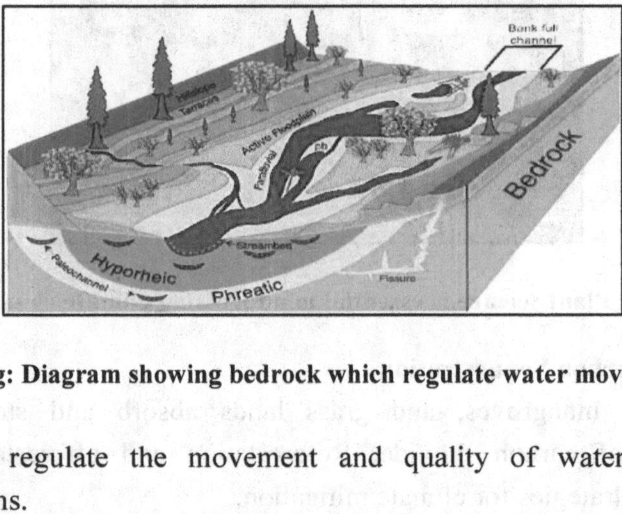

Fig: Diagram showing bedrock which regulate water movement

Plants regulate the movement and quality of water with in ecosystems.

- **Transpiration** contributes to cloud formation and rainfall.
- Vegetations lows water runoff, reducing floods.
- Wetl and plants filter pollutants and improve water quality.

Healthy plant cover is essential for sustainable water management.

9. Conservation Biology and Plant Science

Plant science guides conservation efforts through research and monitoring. Conservation biology and plant science are closely interconnected fields that together address one of the most pressing challenges of the modern world: the loss of biodiversity. Plants form the structural and functional foundation of most ecosystems, and their conservation is essential for the survival of countless other organisms, including humans. Conservation biology applies scientific principles to understand, protect, and manage bio logical diversity, while plant science provides the knowledge needed to study plant diversity, ecology, genetics, and physiology. When combined, these disciplines play a crucial role in safeguarding natural eco systems and promoting sustainable use of plant resources.

Plants are central to biodiversity because they serve as primary producers and habitat providers in ecosystems. They regulate climate, stabilize soils, control water cycles, and support food webs. However, plant species worldwide face increasing threats from habitat destruction, climate change, invasive species, pollution, and over exploitation. Conservation biology seeks to identify these threats and develop strategies to prevent plant extinction, maintain genetic diversity, and restore degraded habitats. Plant science contributes essential tools and insights to these efforts by explaining how plants grow, reproduce, adapt, and respond to environmental stress.

One of the key contributions of plant science to conservation biology is the study of plant diversity and taxonomy. Identifying and classifying plant species is a fundamental step in conservation, as unknown or poorly described species cannot be effectively protected. Many plant species, particularly in tropical regions, remain undiscovered or under-studied. Plant taxonomists help document this diversity, while conservation biologists assess which species are rare, endangered, or at risk of extinction. This information supports the creation of conservation priorities, protected areas, and legal frameworks for plant protection.

Plant ecology is another vital are a linking plant science and conservation biology. Understanding how plants interact with each other, with animals, and with their physical environment helps scientists predict how ecosystems respond to disturbances. For example, knowledge of plant succession—the process by which plant communities change over time—guides habitat restoration projects. Ecological studies also reveal the importance of keystone plant species whose loss can lead to dramatic ecosystem changes. By conserving such species, conservation biologists can protect entire ecosystems rather than focusing on individual organisms alone.

Genetics and biotechnology have become increasingly important in plant conservation. Plant genetic diversity allows species to adapt to changing environments and resist diseases and pests. Conservation biology uses genetic studies to identify small or isolated populations that are at risk of inbreeding and genetic erosion. Plant science provides techniques such as DNA analysis, tissue culture, and seed banking to preserve genetic material. Botanical gardens and seed banks play a crucial role in ex situ conservation, where plants are conserved outside their natural habitats as a safeguard against extinction. Climate change has intensified the need for collaboration between conservation biology and plant science. Rising temperatures, altered rainfall patterns, and extreme weather events are affecting plant growth, distribution, and survival. Plant scientists study how different species respond to these changes at physiological and molecular levels, while conservation biologists use this knowledge to model future scenarios and develop adaptation strategies. Assisted migration, habitat corridors, and climate-resilient restoration projects are examples of conservation approaches informed by plant science research.

Human dependence on plants further emphasizes the importance of their conservation. Plants provide food, medicine, fuel, fiber, and numerous ecosystem services essential for human well- being. Conservation biology promotes the sustainable use of plant resources, ensuring that current needs are met without compromising future generations. Ethno botany, a branch of plant science, documents traditional knowledge about plant uses, helping conserve both biological and cultural diversity. Integrating local communities into conservation efforts increases their effectiveness and long-term success. Education and public awareness are also critical components of conservation biology and plant science. Many people underestimate the importance of plants compared to animals, a phenomenon known as "plant blindness." Through research, outreach, and education, scientists and educators work to highlight the value of plants and the threats they face. Universities, schools, botanical gardens, and conservation organizations play an important role in training future scientists and inspiring public support for plant conservation initiatives.

In conclusion, conservation biology and plant science are deeply interconnected disciplines that together form the backbone of efforts to protect plant diversity and ecosystem health. Plant science provides the fundamental understanding of plant life, while conservation biology applies this knowledge to real-world challenges such as habitat loss, climate change, and species extinction. Protecting plants is not only about preserving nature but also about securing the ecological processes and resources that sustain life on Earth. A strong integration of conservation biology and plant science is essential for achieving a sustainable and resilient future.

9.1. Threats to Plant Diversity

- Deforestation
- Habitat fragmentation
- Invasive species

- Climate change

9.2. Conservation Strategies

- Botanical gardens and seed banks
- Restoration ecology
- Protection of endangered plant species

Scientific knowledge helps design effective conservation policies.

10. Future Role of Plant Science in Sustainability

Advances inplant science will shape the future of sustainable ecosystems.

- Development of climate-resilient crops
- Restoration of degraded ecosystems
- Use of plants in renewable energy and green technologies
- Integration of traditional knowledge with modern science

Plant science bridges ecology, agriculture, and environmental management. Plant science will play decisive role in shapinga sustainable future as the world faces growing challenges such as climate change, population growth, food insecurity, and environmental degradation. Plants form the foundation of life on Earth, and advances in plant science are essential for developing solutions that balance human needs with environmental protection. By improving our understanding of plant biology and applying innovative technologies, plant science can support sustainable development across agriculture, energy, ecosystems, and climate resilience.

One of the most important future contributions of plant science to sustainability lies in sustainable agriculture and food security. With the global population continuing to rise, increasing food production without expanding farmland is a major challenge. Plant science enables the development of high-yielding, climate-resilient crop varieties that require fewer inputs such as water, fertilizers, and pesticides. Through plant breeding, genetics, and biotechnology, scientists can enhance traits such as drought tolerance, disease resistance, and nutrient-use efficiency. These improvements reduce environmental impact while ensuring a stable and nutritious food supply.

Plant science will also be central to addressing climate change. Plants play a key role in regulating the global carbon cycle by absorbing carbon dioxide during photosynthesis and storing it in biomass and soils. Future research aims to improve plants' capacity for carbon sequestration through enhanced root systems, longer-lived vegetation, and improved soil–plant interactions. Restoring forests, grasslands, and mangroves using plant science principles can significantly reduce atmospheric carbon levels while protecting biodiversity and ecosystem services.

Another important area is the development of sustainable bio energy and bio-based materials. Plant science supports the use of renewable plant resources as alternatives to fossil fuels and non-biodegradable materials. Bio fuels derived from crops, algae, and agricultural waste can reduce greenhouse gas emissions when produced responsibly. Additionally, plant-based materials such as bio plastics, natural fibers, and green building materials offer environmentally friendly options that reduce pollution and resource depletion. Advances in plant metabolism and biotechnology will make these alternatives more efficient and economically viable.

Water and soil sustainability will increasingly depend on plant science innovations. Plants influence water cycles by regulating transpiration, improving soil structure, and preventing erosion. Research on drought-tolerant plants, deep-rooted species, and efficient irrigation systems can help conserve water resources in agriculture and urban landscapes. Similarly, plant- based solutions such as phytore mediation use plants to remove pollutants from soil and water, offering cost-effective and eco-friendly methods for environmental cleanup.

Urban sustainability is another area where plant science will have a growing impact. As urban populations expand, green infrastructure such as urban forests, green roofs, and vertical gardens can improve air quality, reduce heat stress, and enhance human well-being. Plant scientists contribute by selecting and developing plant species suited to urban environments, capable of tolerating pollution, limited space, and changing climates. These green solutions help make cities more livable and resilient.

Education, policy, and public engagement will also shape the future role of plant science in sustainability. Translating scientific knowledge into practical applications requires collaboration among scientists, policymakers, farmers, and communities. Plant science education raises awareness of the importance of plants and encourages sustainable practices at individual and societal levels. Evidence-based policies informed by plant research can support conservation, sustainable agriculture, and climate adaptation strategies.

In conclusion, plant science will be a corner stone of global sustainability efforts in the future. By enhancing food security, mitigating climate change, supporting renewable resources, and restoring ecosystems, plant science provides powerful tools for building a resilient and sustainable world. Continued investment in plant research, education, and innovation is essential to ensure that plants continue to sustain life on Earth for generations to come.

Multiple Choice Questions (MCQs)

1. Which of the following is the primary role of plants in a sustainable ecosystem?

a) Decomposers
b) Consumers
c) Primary Producers
d) Predators

2. What is the process by which plants reduce atmospheric and help mitigate climate change?

a) Respiration
b) Carbon Sequestration
c) Transpiration
d) Decomposition

3. The use of plants to clean up polluted soil or water is known as:

a) Phytoremediation
b) Photosynthesis
c) Afforestation
d) Cultivation

4. Which of the following is a plant-derived method for soil conservation?

a) Overgrazing
b) Deforestation
c) Root binding
d) Industrialization

5. What is the primary nutrient fixed by Rhizobium in a symbiotic relationship with plants?

a) Oxygen
b) Nitrogen
c) Carbon
d) Hydrogen

6. Which type of plant is most suitable for restoring degraded land?

a) Invasive species
b) Annual crops
c) Pioneer species

d) Exotic species

7. Sustainable agriculture relies on which practice to maintain soil fertility?

a) High chemical fertilizer use

b) Crop rotation

c) Monoculture

d) Deep plowing

8. Plants play a key role in the hydrological cycle through:

a) Respiration

b) Transpiration

c) Photosynthesis

d) Germination

9. Biodiversity hotspots are mainly characterized by high levels of:

a) Urbanization

b) Industrial pollution

c) Endemic plant species

d) Soil erosion

10. Which of the following is a sustainable approach to forest management?

a) Clear-cutting

b) Afforestation

c) Monoculture farming

d) Deforestation

Vedantu +5

Descriptive Type Questions

1. Explain how plants act as the foundation of energy flow in a terrestrial ecosystem.

2. Describe the role of plant roots in preventing soil erosion and improving soil structure.

3. Discuss the mechanism of phytoremediation and give an example of a plant used to clean heavy metal contamination.

4. How do forests contribute to climate regulation through carbon sequestration?

5. Explain the significance of genetic diversity in plants for developing climate-resilient crops.

6. Describe the symbiotic relationship between leguminous plants and nitrogen-fixing bacteria, and its importance for sustainable agriculture.

7. What is the role of plants in the water cycle, and how does deforestation affect local rainfall patterns?

8. Discuss the concept of "functional biodiversity" in ecosystems and how plant diversity supports it.

9. Explain the importance of conserving native plant species for ecosystem stability.

10. How can biotechnology in plant science contribute to achieving food security in a sustainable manner?

Chapter 3

Medicinal and economic Importance of Plants

Dr Geetika Singh
Assistant professor, dept of basic and applied sciences, madhav university sirohi

Medicinal and Economic Importance of Plants

Plants are foundational to life on Earth. They sustain ecosystems, provide oxygen, and form the basis of food webs. Beyond these ecological roles, plants are integral to human health and the economy. Humans have used plants for medicines, food, fuel, fibers, and much more across cultures and centuries. This chapter explores how plants contribute to medicine, industry, and economic development, blending science with real-world examples. Medicinal and Economic Importance of Plants. Plants have been essential to human survival and development since the beginning of civilization. They provide not only food and shelter but also medicines and raw materials that support economies around the world. The medicinal and economic importance of plants highlights their value beyond ecological functions, demonstrating their direct contribution to human health, livelihoods, and sustainable development.

The medicinal importance of plants is one of their most significant contributions to humanity. For thousands of years, plants have been used in traditional systems of medicine such as Ayurveda, Traditional Chinese Medicine, Unani, and various indigenous healing practices. These systems rely on plant parts such as leaves, roots, bark, seeds, and flowers to treat diseases and maintain health. Even today, a large proportion of the world's population depends on plant-based medicines for primary healthcare, especially in developing regions where access to modern medical facilities may be limited.

Many modern pharmaceutical drugs are derived directly or indirectly from plants. For example, aspirin was developed from salicylic acid found in willow bark, quinine used to treat malaria comes from the cinchona tree, and morphine is derived from the opium poppy. Plants contain a wide range of bioactive compounds, including alkaloids, flavonoids, terpenoids, and glycosides, which have therapeutic properties such as antibacterial, anti-inflammatory, anticancer, and antioxidant effects. Ongoing research in plant science and pharmacology continues to discover new medicinal compounds, highlighting the importance of conserving plant biodiversity.

In addition to medicine, plants have immense economic importance. Agriculture forms the backbone of many national economies and depends entirely on plant cultivation. Crops such as rice, wheat, maize, and pulses provide staple foods, while fruits and vegetables contribute to nutrition and food security. Cash crops like cotton, sugarcane, tea, coffee, cocoa, and rubber generate income, support trade, and provide employment to millions of people worldwide. The economic stability of many rural communities is closely linked to plant-based agriculture.

Plants are also a major source of raw materials for industries. Timber from trees is used in construction, furniture making, and paper production. Plant fibers such as cotton, jute, flax, and hemp are essential for the textile industry. Oils extracted from plants like sunflower, coconut, mustard, and oil pal mare used for cooking, cosmetics, soaps, and bio fuels. Spices, herbs, and condiments derived from plants contribute significantly to global trade and cultural cuisines, adding both economic and social value.

The role of plants in the medicinal and economic sectors also extends to emerging industries. Herbal medicine, nutraceuticals, and plant-based cosmetics are rapidly growing markets driven by increased consumer interest in natural and sustainable products.

Essential oils from plants such as lavender, eucalyptus, and pepper mintare widely use dinaroma therapy, pharmaceuticals, and personal care products. These industries create employment opportunities and promote sustainable use of plant resources when managed responsibly.

Despite their immense value, medicinal and economically important plants face serious threats from overharvesting, habitat loss, and climate change. Un sustainable exploitation can lead to the decline or extinction of valuable plant species, reducing future benefits. Conservation and sustainable management practices are therefore essential to protect these resources. Cultivation of medicinal plants, regulation of trade, and scientific research can help ensure that plant resources remain available for future generations.

In conclusion, plants hold tremendous medicinal and economic importance, forming the basis of healthcare systems, agriculture, industry, and trade. They provide life-saving drugs, support livelihoods, and drive economic growth while offering sustainable alternatives to synthetic products. Recognizing and protecting the value of plants is crucialnot only for human well-being but also for long-term environmental and economic sustainability.

1. **Introduction: Why Plants Matter**

Fig: Plants showing bio active components and formation of extracts

Plants are far more than green scenery—they are sources of **bioactive compounds** used in traditional and modern medicine, feed live stock and people, produce raw materials for industries, and contribute to global trade. The study of plant uses in human society is known as **ethnobotany** or **economic botany.**

2. Medicinal Importance of Plants

2.1. Historical Background

Plants have been used medicinally since prehistoric times. Ancient civilizations, including those in India, China, Egypt, Greece, and the Americas, developed detailed herbal pharmacopoeias:

- **Ayurveda (India)**: Described plant-based treatments for thousands of years.
- **Traditional Chinese Medicine (TCM)**: Relies on herbs such as ginseng and astragalus.

These traditions laid foundations for modern pharmacology.

2.2. Bioactive Compounds in Plants

Plants synthesize **secondary metabolites**—compounds not directly involved in growth but vital for survival (e.g., defense against pathogens). Many of these compounds have therapeutic value:

Key categories include:

- **Alkaloids**–Often have strong physiological effects (e.g., morphine, quinine).
- **Flavonoids** – Antioxidants found in many fruits and herbs.
- **Terpenoids**–Contribute to aromatic properties and therapeutic effects (e.g., menthol).
- **Glycosides**–Cardiac glycosides (e.g., digitalis) regulate heart function.

2.3. Examples of Medicinal Plants and Uses

Below are not able medicinal plants with their key therapeutic roles:

2.3.1. Willow (Salixspp.)

Fig: Diagram showing plant body of willow and its active constituents

- **Importance**: Source of **salicin**, historically used for pain and fever.
- **Modern medicine**: Salicinled to the development of **aspirin**.

2.3.2. Digitalis (Fox glove)

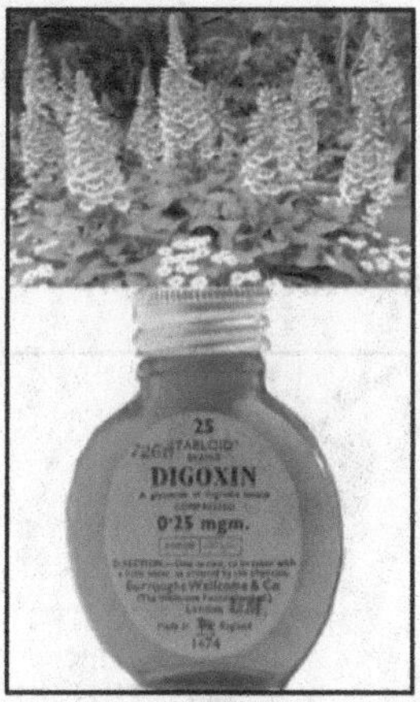

Figure:Activeconstituentindigitalis

- **Active compounds**: Cardiac glycosides (e.g., digoxin).
- **Use**: Strengthens heart contractions; used in certain heart conditions.

2.3.3. Turmeric (Curcumalonga)

Figure:Activeandkeycomponentofturmeric

- **Key compound**: **Curcumin** —anti-inflammatory and antioxidant.
- **Uses**: Traditional anti-inflammatory tonic; studied for potential therapeutic roles.

2.3.4. Cinchona (Cinchonaspp.)

Fig: Active component of Cinchona

- **Active compound**: **Quinine**—used to treat malaria.
- **Impact**: Changed the course of tropical medicine.

2.3.5. Aloe (Aloevera)

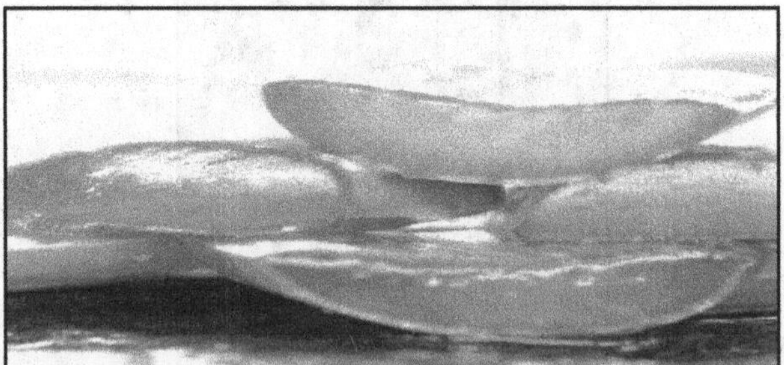

Fig: Active component of Aloevera

- **Uses**: Soothes burns, moisturizes skin, digestive health remedies.
- **Market**: Widely used in cosmetics and health products.

2.4. From Traditional Knowledge to Modern Drugs

Many plant compounds serve as proto types for synthetic drugs. For example:

- **Paclitaxel (Taxol)** from the Pacificyew tree—used in cancer therapy.
- **Morphine** from opiumpoppy — revolution izedpain management.
- **Atropine**, sourced from deadly night shade—use dineye and cardiac treatments.

Such transitions illustrate how traditional herbal medicine informs modern pharmacology.

2.5. Challenges and Ethical Considerations

Medicinal plant use also raises challenges:

- **Over harvesting** threatens wild populations of high-value plants.
- **Bio piracy**—when corporations patent traditional knowledge without fair compensation.
- **Safety and Standardization**—herbal products vary inpotency and purity.

Conservation and ethical frameworks are necessary toprotect both biodiversity and cultural heritage.

3. Economic Importance of Plants

Beyond medicine, plants are in dispensable to global economies. They support industries such as agriculture, forestry, textiles, pharmaceuticals, and tourism.

3.1. Food and Agriculture

Plantsprovidethe**primarysourceofcalories**forhumansandlivestock. Majorfoodplants include cereals (wheat, rice, maize), legumes (beans, peas), fruits, and vegetables.

3.1.1. Staple Crops

- **Rice** (Oryzasativa) feeds billions, especially in Asia.
- **Wheat** (Triticumaestivum) is as taple in Europe, the Middle East.
- **Maize** (Zeamays) is a staple in the Americas and Africa.

These crops form the back bone of food security and livelihoods globally.

3.2. Industrial Raw Materials

Plants supply materials for energy and manufacturing:

3.2.1. Timber and Wood Products

Fig: Diagram showing timber and its products

- **Uses**: Construction, furniture, paper, fuel wood.
- **Economic impact**: Forestry supports jobs and exports.

3.2.2. Fibers

Fig: Diagram showing fibres and its products

Plants produce key fibers for textiles:

- **Cotton**—dominant natural fiber worldwide.
- **Flax**—used to make linen.
- **Jute and hemp**—strong fibers for ropes and sacks.

These industries support global trade and manufacturing.

3.3. Oils and Bio fuels

Plants are sources of edible oil sand renewable energy.

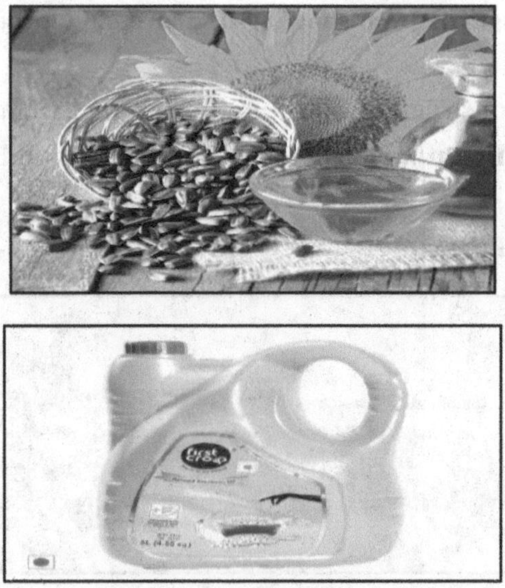

Fig: Diagram showing plant with its active constituent with edible oil

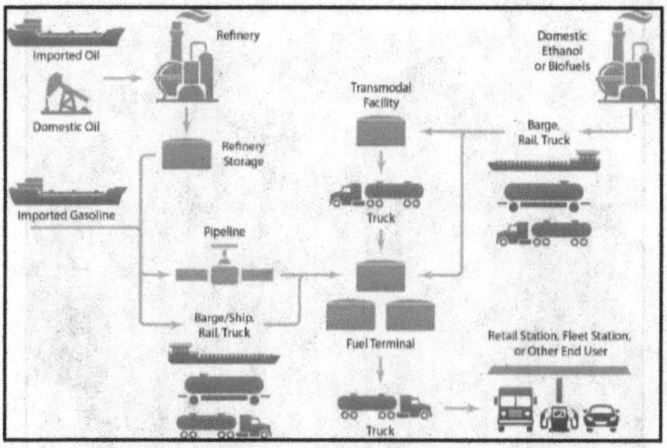

Fig: Flow chart showing active constituent inplants and its use in sustainable energy

- **Edible oils**: Sunflower, soybean, palm—important for nutrition and cooking industries.
- **Bio fuels**: Plants such as sugarcane and maize produce ethanol, a renewable fuel alternative.

The plant-based energy sector is growing as countries seeks stainable energy.

3.4. Ornamental and Cultural Value

Plants enhance landscapes, gardens, and cultural practices:

Fig: Diagram showing ornamental value of plants

- **Flowers** like roses, orchids, tulips are economically significant in floriculture.
- **Cultural roles**: Plants feature in festivals, rituals, and traditional crafts.

These sectors support tourism and local economies.

4. Case Studies in Economic Botany

4.1. The Spice Trade

Fig: Diagram showing various spices

Spices such as **pepper, cinnamon, nutmeg, and cloves** drove global trade for centuries. They were valuable enough to shape exploration, colonialism, and world commerce.

4.2. Tea and Coffee Economies

Fig: Diagram showing agricultural land with tea and coffee plantations

Fig: Diagram showing active constituent in tea and coffee

- **Tea (Camellia sinensis)** and **coffee (Coffea Arabica & robusta)** are among the most traded agricultural commodities.
- Entire regions depend on these cash crops for jobs and foreign exchange.

5. Conservation and Sustainable Use

Medicinal plants are vital resources that have sustained human health for centuries. They provide the raw materials for traditional medicines, modern pharmaceuticals, nutraceuticals, and herbal products. However, the increasing demand for medicinal plants, coupled with habitat destruction, overharvesting, and climate change, has put many species at risk. Conservation and sustainable use of medicinal plants are therefore critical to ensure their availability for future generations while maintaining ecological balance. Medicinal plants are harvested from the wild for their therapeutic properties. Leaves, roots, bark, seeds, and flowers contain bioactive compounds used in treating a wide range of ailments. For centuries, indigenous communities have relied on these plants for primary healthcare, while modern medicine continues to extract compounds for drugs such as morphine, quinine, and paclitaxel. The growing popularity of herbal remedies and plant-based products has significantly increased the pressure on natural populations. Unsustainable collection, particularly of roots and bark, often damages or kills the plant, threatening species survival.

Habitat destruction is another major factor endangering medicinal plants. Deforestation, urbanization, agricultural expansion, and mining reduce the natural areas where these plants grow. Many medicinal plants have specific ecological requirements, and the loss of their habitat can lead to population decline or extinction. Climate change further exacerbates this problem by altering rainfall patterns, temperatures, and soil conditions, making it difficult for certain species to survive in their native habitats.

Conservation strategies for medicinal plants involve both in situ and ex situ approaches. **In situ conservation** focuses on protecting plants in their natural habitats. This includes establishing protected areas such as national parks, biosphere reserves, and sacred groves where medicinal plants can grow without human interference. Community-led conservation efforts, where local people participate in monitoring and protecting plant populations, have proven particularly effective. These approaches not only safeguard plant diversity but also maintain the ecological processes necessary for their growth.

Exsituconservationinvolvespreservingplantsoutsidetheirnaturalha bitats.Botanicalgardens, seed banks, and tissue culture facilities play a crucial role in ex situ conservation. Seed banks store seeds under controlled conditions, maintaining genetic diversity and allowing for future reintroduction programs. Tissue culture and micro propagation techniques enable rapid multiplication of rare or slow-growing species without removing large numbers of plants from the wild. This reduces the pressure on natural populations while ensuring a steady supply of medicinal plants for research, pharmaceutical use, and cultivation.

Sustainable harvesting practices are essential to balance utilization and conservation. These include rotational harvesting, collecting only certain plant parts, and leaving enough mature plants to reproduce. Cultivation of medicinal plants is another effective strategy to meet demand without depleting wild populations. Many medicinal plants, such as ashwagandha, aloevera, turmeric, and neem, can be successfully grown under controlled agricultural conditions. Cultivational so provides economic opportunities for farmers, encouraging them to protect rather than exploit wild populations.

Education and awareness play a critical role in conservation. Training local communities, herbal practitioners, and traders about sustainable collection techniques and the ecological importance of medicinal plants ensures that harvesting practices are responsible and ethical. Government policies and international agreements, such as the Convention on Biological Diversity (CBD), provide legal frameworks for protecting medicinal plant species and promoting sustainable use. Certification schemes for sustainably sourced plant products can further support conservation efforts.

In conclusion, the conservation and sustainable use of medicinal plants are essential for ecological stability, human health, and economic development. Protecting wild populations through in situ and ex situ strategies, promoting cultivation, applying sustainable harvesting practices, and raising awareness all contribute to preserving these invaluable resources. By integrating scientific knowledge, community participation, and responsible policies, we can ensure that medicinal plants continue to benefit humanity while maintaining the balance of natural ecosystems.

While plants offer immense benefits, **unsustainable practices** threaten biodiversity:

5.1. Over exploitation

Medicinal plants like wild ginseng, certain orchids, and slow-growing trees face risk from overharvesting.

5.2. Habitat Loss

Agricultural expansion, urbanization, and climate change reduce natural habitats.

5.3. Conservation Strategies

- **Protected are as and botanical gardens** safeguard species.
- **Sustainable harvesting protocols** balance use with regeneration.
- **Bio technological tools** (tissueculture, seedbanks) preserve genetic diversity.

6. Future Prospects and Research

Scientific advances continue to unlock plant potential:

- **Phyto pharmaceuticals**—new drugs derived from plants.

- **Genetic improvement**—higher yields, disease resistance.
- **Green chemistry**—plant-based materials replace petrochemicals.
- **Agro forestry and sustainable agriculture** integrate crops and forestry for resilient landscapes.

Ongoing research bridges traditional knowledge with modern science to meet global health and sustainability goals.

Multiple Choice questions

1. Which branch of science specifically studies plants?

A. Zoology

B. Ecology

C. Botany

D. Microbiology

2. What is the primary process by which green plants contribute to sustainability?

A. Respiration

B. Transpiration

C. Photosynthesis

D. Fermentation

3. During photosynthesis, plants absorb which gas from the atmosphere?

A. Oxygen

B. Nitrogen

C. Carbon dioxide

D. Hydrogen

4. Which plant component plays a major role in preventing soil erosion?

A. Flowers

B. Fruits

C. Roots

D. Leaves

5. Nitrogen-fixing bacteria are commonly found in the roots of:

A. Ferns

B. Mosses

C. Leguminous plants

D. Algae

6. Which of the following best describes biodiversity?

A. Number of animals in a zoo

B. Variety of life forms in an ecosystem

C. Study of rocks

D. Weather patterns over time

7. Plants help regulate the water cycle mainly through:

A. Germination

B. Pollination

C. Transpiration

D. Fertilization

8. Sustainable agriculture primarily aims to:

A. Maximize short-term profits

B. Use unlimited chemical fertilizers

C. Maintain productivity without harming the environment

D. Eliminate all insects

9. Which ecosystem service is directly provided by forests?

A. Plastic production

B. Carbon sequestration

C. Oil refining

D. Mining

10. Conservation of native plant species is important because it:

A. Reduces oxygen production

B. Decreases biodiversity

C. Supports ecosystem stability

D. Prevents rainfall

Here are **10 descriptive-type questions** on Plants and Their Role in a Sustainable Ecosystem

1. Explain how photosynthesis contributes to maintaining ecological balance and reducing climate change.

2. Discuss the role of plants in the carbon cycle and how they help in carbon sequestration.

3. Describe how plant root systems help in preventing soil erosion and maintaining soil fertility.

4. Explain the importance of plants in supporting biodiversity within an ecosystem.

5. Discuss the role of forests in regulating the water cycle and maintaining rainfall patterns.

6. Describe how plants contribute to sustainable agriculture and food security.

7. Explain the relationship between plants and pollinators and its importance for ecosystem sustainability.

8. Discuss the role of native plant species in maintaining ecosystem stability and resilience.

9. Explain how deforestation affects ecosystem sustainability and climate balance.

10. Describe the importance of afforestation and reforestation in restoring degraded ecosystems.

Chapter 4

Applied Mathematics in Climate Change and Environmental Sustainability

Mohd Farman Ali
Professor, Dept of Mathematics, Madhav University, Sirohi

2.1 Introduction

Climate change and environmental sustainability have emerged as defining challenges of the modern world. Rapid industrialization, urban expansion, deforestation, and exces-sive consumption of natural resources have significantly altered Earth's climate system. Rising global temperatures, melting glaciers, sea-level rise, extreme weather events, and biodiversity loss pose serious threats to human societies and natural ecosystems alike.

Applied mathematics plays a fundamental role in understanding, analyzing, and ad- dressing these challenges. Mathematical techniques provide the quantitative foundation required to model climate systems, analyze environmental data, assess risks, and de-sign sustainable policies. Through mathematical modeling, scientists can simulate future climate scenarios, evaluate mitigation strategies, and optimize resource management.

This chapter explores the application of mathematic sin climate change studies and en- vironmental sustainability. Emphasis is placed on mathematical models, analytical tools, optimization methods, and uncertainty analysis that contribute to informed decision- making and long-term ecological balance.

2.2 Role of Mathematics in Climate Science

Climate science involves the study of complex interactions among the atmosphere, oceans, cryosphere, biosphere, and human activities. These interactions operate across multiple spatial and temporal scales, making direct experimentation impractical. Mathematics provides a systematic framework to integrate physical laws, observational data, and com-Putational methods.

Mathematical model sin climate science serve several key purposes:

- Understanding climate mechanisms and feedback processes
- Predicting future climate trends
- Assessing the impact of anthropogenic activities
- Supporting climate policy and adaptation planning

2.2.1 Climate Variables and Parameters

Key variables commonly used in climate models include atmospheric temperature, carbon dioxide concentration, ocean heat content,ice cover, and surface albedo. Parameters represent physical constants or empirical coefficients governing system behavior.

2.3 Energy Balance Models

Energy balance models (EBMs) represent one of the simplest mathematical approaches to climate modeling. These models are based on the principle of conservation of energy, equating incoming solar radiation with outgoing terrestrial radiation.

2.3.1 Global Energy Balance Equation

The basic form of a global energy balance model is given by:

$$(1 - \alpha) S = \epsilon\sigma T4 \quad (2.1)$$

where S is the solar constant, α is the planetary albedo, ϵ is the emissivity of Earth's surface, σ is the Stefan–Boltzmann constant, and T is the global mean surface tempera- ture.

This equation illustrates how changes in albedo or greenhouse gas concentration can significantly affect Earth's temperature.

2.3.2 Time-Dependent Energy Balance Model

A more realistic model incorporates emporal variation:

$$C\, dT = (1 - \alpha)S - \epsilon\sigma T\, 4 \qquad (2.2)$$

dt

where C denotes the effective heat capacity of the climate system.

2.4 Mathematical Modeling of the Carbon Cycle

The carbon cycle plays a central role in climate change, governing the exchange of carbon among the atmosphere, oceans, land, and biosphere. Mathematical models help quantify these exchanges and predict future atmospheric carbon levels.

2.4.1 Atmospheric Carbon Concentration Model

A simplified carbon balance equationis:

$$\frac{dC}{dt} = E(t) - kC \qquad (2.3)$$

where C(t) represents atmospheric carbon concentration, E(t) denotes anthropogenic emissions, and k is the natural removal rate due to absorption by oceans and vegetation.

2.4.2 Interpretation and Implications

This model highlights the importance of emission reduction strategies. If emissions ex-ceed natural absorption capacity, atmospheric carbon levels increase, intensifying global warming.

2.5 Differential Equation Models in Climate Dynam-ics

Many climate processes are governed by differential equations derived from physical laws such as conservation of mass, momentum, and energy.

2.5.1 Temperature Diffusion Model

Spatial temperature distribution can be modeled using a diffusion equation:

$$\frac{\partial T}{\partial t} = \kappa \nabla 2T + Q \qquad (2.4)$$

Where κ is the ther mal diffusivity and Q represents external heat sources.

2.5.2 Ocean Circulation Models

Ocean currents transport heat across the globe and significantly influence climate pat- terns. Mathematical models of ocean circulation involve systems of nonlinear partial differential equations.

2.6 Mathematics in Environmental Sustainability

Environmental sustainability focuses on meeting present needs without compromising the ability of future generations to meet their own needs. Mathematics supports sustainability through resource modeling, impact assessment, and optimization.

2.6.1 Renewable Resource Models

Renewable resources such as forests and fisheries can be modeled using logistic growth with harvesting:

$dR = rR1 - R - H$ (2.5)

where R(t) is the resource stock, r is the intrinsic growth rate, K is the carrying capacity, and H is the harvesting rate.

2.6.2 Sustainable Harvesting

Sustainable management requires choosing H such that the resource remains stable over time. Mathematical analysis helps determine optimal harvesting policies.

2.7 Optimization Techniques in Environmental Pol-icy

Optimization plays a crucial role in balancing economic development with environmental protection.

2.7.1 Cost–Benefit Optimization

A typical environmental optimization problem is: min

x

$C(x)$ subject to $E(x) \leq E_{max}$ (2.6)

where C(x) represents economic cost and E(x) denotes environmental impact.

2.7.2 Linear and Non linear Programming

Many sustainability problems involve linear or non linear programming techniques, en- abling policymakers to evaluate trade-offs among competing objectives.

2.8 Stochastic Models and Climate Uncertainty

Climate predictions are inherently uncertain due to variability innatural processes and limitations in data. Stochastic models incorporate randomness to represent uncertainty.

2.8.1 Stochastic Temperature Model

Asto chastic differential equation for temperature evolutionis:

$dT=\mu(T,t)\,dt+\sigma(T,t)\,dW_t$ (2.7) where W_t isa Wiener process.

2.8.2 Risk Assessment

Probabilistic models help estimate the likelihood of extreme climate events and guide risk-informed decision-making.

2.9 Case Study: Emission Reduction Strategies

Consider a region aiming to reduce car bone missions while maintaining economic growth. Let E (t) represent emissions and G (t) economic output. An optimization model can be formulated to minimize emissions subject to growth constraints. Mathematical solutions provide insights into feasible and efficient policy pathways.

2.10 Figures and Illustrations

Global Energy Balance Diagram

Figure2.1: Simplified Representation of Earth's Energy Balance

Carbon Cycle Flowchart

Figure2.2: Major Carbon Reservoirs and Fluxes

2.11 Advantages and Limitations of Mathematical Models

2.11.1 Advantages

- Enable quantitative analysis of climate scenarios
- Support long-term sustainability planning
- Assist policy makers with evidence-based decisions

2.11.2 Limitations

- Dependence on assumptions and parameter estimates
- Computational complexity of large-scale models
- Uncertainty in long-term predictions

2.12 Recent Developments

Recent advances include high-resolution climate simulations, data-driven modeling, and integration of machine learning with traditional mathematical approaches. These devel-opments enhance predictive accuracy and improve understanding of complex environ-mental systems.

2.13 Conclusion

Applied mathematics is indispensable in addressing climate changeand promoting en-vironmental sustainability. Mathematical models provide critical insights into climate dynamics, resource management, and policy design. As environmental challenges con-tinue to intensify, the integration of advanced mathematical methods with environmental science will remain essential for achieving a sustainable future.

Multiple Choice Questions (MCQs)

1. Which mathematical method is commonly used to predict long-term climate patterns?

A. Linear equations

B. Differential equations
C. Matrix inversion
D. Number theory

Answer: B. Differential equations

2. Climate models often use numerical methods to approximate solutions of:

A. Algebraic identities
B. Differential equations
C. Probability axioms
D. Geometry theorems

Answer: B. Differential equations

3. The concept of feedback loops in climate systems is commonly analyzed using:

A. Graph theory
B. Dynamical systems
C. Number theory
D. Set theory

Answer: B. Dynamical systems

4. Which statistical method is widely used to analyze temperature trends over time?

A. Regression analysis
B. Vector calculus
C. Topology
D. Cryptography

Answer: A. Regression analysis

5. Mathematical models that simulate Earth's climate are called:

A. Climate projections
B. Climate algorithms
C. Climate models
D. Climate formulas

Answer: C. Climate models

6. Which mathematical tool helps estimate uncertainty in climate predictions?

A. Probability theory

B. Graph theory

C. Geometry

D. Arithmetic

Answer: A. Probability theory

7. Optimization techniques in environmental sustainability are used to:

A. Maximize pollution

B. Minimize resource use and environmental impact

C. Increase energy consumption

D. Reduce mathematical complexity

Answer: B. Minimize resource use and environmental impact

8. Population models used in environmental studies are often based on:

A. Logarithmic growth equations

B. Logistic growth equations

C. Trigonometric identities

D. Polynomial division

Answer: B. Logistic growth equations

9. Which mathematical approach helps simulate the spread of pollutants in air or water?

A. Differential equations

B. Geometry

C. Number theory

D. Statistics only

Answer: A. Differential equations

10. Monte Carlo simulations are mainly used for:

A. Exact solutions

B. Randomized modeling and prediction
C. Graph drawing
D. Algebraic simplification
Answer: B. Randomized modeling and prediction

Descriptive Questions

1. Explain the role of Applied Mathematics in understanding and predicting climate change.
2. Describe how differential equations are used in climate models to represent atmospheric and ocean dynamics.
3. Discuss the importance of mathematical modeling in achieving environmental sustainability.
4. Explain the concept of feedback mechanisms in climate systems and how they are represented mathematically.
5. Describe how statistical analysis helps in detecting long-term climate trends.
6. Explain how optimization techniques can help design sustainable energy systems.
7. Discuss the role of probability and uncertainty analysis in climate change predictions.
8. Explain how mathematical models are used to study the spread of pollutants in the environment.
9. Describe how population growth models contribute to environmental sustainability planning.
10. Discuss the limitations of mathematical models in predicting climate change and environmental impacts

Chapter 5

Networks, Graph Theory, and the Structure of Modern Society

Mohd Farman Ali
Professor, Dept of Mathematics, Madhav University, Sirohi

1.1 Introduction

Modern society is fundamentally shaped by networks. Social interactions, communica-tion systems, transportation infrastructures, biological systems, and digital platforms all exhibit net worked structures. Graph theory provides a rigorous mathematical framework for representing and analyzing such networks. Through nodes and edges, graph theory captures relationships, interactions, and flows that define the structure and function of complex systems.

In recent decades, the study of networks has evolved into a multidisciplinary field known as network science. Mathematical analysis of networks has transformed our un- derstanding of social connectivity, information diffusion, economic systems, epidemiology, and technological infrastructures. This chapter introduces the fundamental concepts of graph theory and explores their applications in modeling the structure of modern society.

1.2 Historical Development of Graph Theory

Graph theory originated in the eighteenth century with Leonhard Euler's solution to the Ko¨nigsberg bridge problem. Euler's work marked the first formal study of a network structure using mathematical reasoning. Over time, graph theory developed as a branch of discrete mathematics with applications in chemistry, operations research, and computer science. In the late twentieth century, advances in computing and data availability enabled large-scale network analysis. Social networks, the Internet, and biological networks be-came central objects of study, leading to the emergence of modern network science.

1.3 Basic Concepts of Graph Theory

1.3.1 Graph

A graph Gisan ordered pair G=(V,E), where Visan on-empty set of vertices (nodes) and Eisa set of edges representing connections between vertices.

1.3.2 Types of Graphs

- Undirected graph: Edges have no orientation.
- Directed graph(digraph):Edges have direction.
- Weighted graph: Edges are assigned weights.
- Simple graph: No loops or multipleedges.

1.3.3 Degree of a Vertex

The degree of a vertex is the number of edges incident to it. Indirected graphs, in-degree and out-degree are defined separately.

1.4 Mathematical Representation of Networks

1.4.1 Adjacency Matrix

A graph withn vertices can be represented by an adjacency matrix A= [aij], where:

aij

= [illegible] if there is an edge between i and j 0, otherwise

(3.1)

1.4.2 Adjacency List

An adjacency list represents a graph as a collection of lists, where each vertex stores its neighboring vertices. This representation is efficient for sparse networks.

1.5 Classical Graph Models

1.5.1 Random Graphs

The Erdo″s–R′enyi model assumes that edges between pairs of vertices exist with a fixed probability p. Such models help analyze randomness and connectivity in large networks.

1.5.2 Small-World Networks

Small-world networks exhibit high clustering and short average path lengths. These net- works are common in social systems, where individuals are connected through surprisingly short chains.

1.5.3 Scale-Free Networks

Scale-free networks are characterized by power-law degree distributions. A small number of nodes, known as hubs, have disproportionately large numbers of connections. Examples include the Internet and social media platforms.

1.6 Social Networks and Society

Social networks represent individuals as nodes and social relationships as edges. Graph theory enables the quantitative analysis of social structure, influence, and cohesion.

1.6.1 Measures of Centrality

Important centrality measures include:

- Degree centrality
- Betweenness centrality
- Closeness centrality
- Eigenvector centrality

These measures identify influential individuals within a social network.

1.6.2 Community Detection

Communities are groups of nodes with dense internal connections. Mathematical algo-rithms such as modularity optimization are used to detect communities in large networks.

1.7 Information Diffusion and Spread

Graph theory provides tools to model the spread of information, ideas, and behaviors in society.

1.7.1 Diffusion Model

Let xi (t) denote the state of node I at time t. A simple diffusion model is:

Xi (t+1) = j∈N(i) wijxj(t) (3.2)

Where N (i) is the neighborhood of node i and w_{ij} are influence weights.

1.7.2 Applications

Such models are used to study viral marketing, rumor spreading, and opinion dynamics.

1.8 Networks in Economics and Infrastructure

Economic systems can be modeled as networks of agents, firms, or markets. Transporta- tion and power grids are also naturally represented as graphs.

1.8.1 Flow Networks

In flow networks, edges have capacities, and mathematical optimization determines max- imum flow:

Maximize Σfij (3.3)

Subject to capacity and conservation constraints.

1.9 Epidemic Spreadon Networks

Disease transmission depends strongly on network structure. Graph-based epidemic mod- els provide more realistic predictions than homogeneous mixing models.

1.9.1 Network-Based SIR Model

Each node represents an individual, and disease spreads along edges. The probability of infection depends on network connectivity and transmission rates.

1.10 Technological and Digital Networks

The Internet, social media platforms, and communication systems are examples of large- scale technological networks.

1.10.1 Internet as a Graph

Routers and servers act as nodes, while communication links form edges. Graph theory helps analyze robustness, vulnerability, and efficiency.

1.11 Figures and Illustrations

Social Network Graph

Figure3.1: Example of a Social Network Structure

Scale-Free Network

Figure3.2: Illustration of a Scale-Free Network with Hubs

1.12 Advantages and Limitations of Network Models

1.12.1 Advantages

- Capture complex relational structures
- Applicable across disciplines
- Enable quantitative analysis of connectivity and influence

1.12.2 Limitations

- Data availability and accuracy
- Over simplification of human behavior
- Computational challenges for large networks

1.13 Recent Developments in Network Science

Recent research focuses on multilayer networks, temporal networks, and data-driven net- work modeling. These approaches provide deeper insights into evolving social and tech-nological systems.

1.14 Conclusion

Graph theory and network analysis offer powerful mathematical tools for understanding the structure and dynamics of modern society. By representing complex systems as networks, researchers can analyze connectivity, resilience, and information flow across social, economic, and technological domains. As data availability and computational power increase, network-based approaches will continue to play a vital role in addressing contemporary societal challenges.

Multiple Choice Questions (MCQs)

1. In **Graph Theory**, a **vertex** represents:

A. A connection between nodes

B. A node or entity in the network

C. A path in the graph

D. A direction of flow

Answer: B. A node or entity in the network

2. The connection between two vertices in a graph is called:

A. Edge

B. Matrix

C. Vector

D. Loop

Answer: A. Edge

3. A graph where edges have directions is known as:

A. Undirected graph

B. Directed graph

C. Weighted graph

D. Simple graph

Answer: B. Directed graph

4. In social network analysis, individuals are represented as:

A. Edges

B. Vertices (nodes)

C. Paths

D. Cycles

Answer: B. Vertices (nodes)

5. Which concept measures the number of connections a node has?

A. Degree

B. Diameter

C. Cycle

D. Path

Answer: A. Degree

6. A graph with no cycles is called a:

A. Network

B. Tree

C. Complete graph

D. Weighted graph

Answer: B. Tree

7. Which measure identifies the most influential nodes in a network?

A. Centrality

B. Density

C. Symmetry

D. Balance

Answer: A. Centrality

8. A network where every pair of vertices is connected by an edge is called:

A. Sparse graph

B. Complete graph

C. Cyclic graph

D. Directed graph

Answer: B. Complete graph

9. The shortest route between two nodes in a network is called:

A. Cycle

B. Path

C. Shortest path

D. Edge

Answer: C. Shortest path

10. Graph theory is commonly used to analyze which modern system?

A. Social media networks

B. Transportation systems

C. Communication networks

D. All of the above

Answer: D. All of the above

Descriptive Questions

1. Explain the basic concepts of **Graph Theory**, including vertices and edges.

2. Describe how **Network Science** helps in understanding the structure of modern societies.

3. Discuss the role of graph theory in analyzing social networks and online communities.

4. Explain the concept of centrality and its importance in identifying influential individuals in networks.

5. Describe different types of graphs (directed, undirected, weighted) with examples.

6. Explain how graph theory is used in transportation and communication networks.

7. Discuss the importance of shortest path algorithms in network analysis.

8. Explain how network models help understand the spread of information or diseases in society.

9. Discuss the applications of graph theory in technology, including the internet and social media platforms.

10. Explain the limitations and challenges of using network models to represent real-world social systems.

Chapter 6

Mathematical Modeling of Social and Natural Systems

1.1 Introduction

Mathematical modeling is a powerful interdisciplinary tool that allows researchers to represent, analyze, and predict the behavior of complex systems arising in social and natural contexts. Social systems such as population growth, spread of information, eco- nomic interactions, and opinion dynamics, as well as natural systems including ecological interactions, climate processes, and epidemiological phenomena, are often characterized by nonlinearity, uncertainty, and feedback mechanisms. Mathematics provides a struc-tured language to translate these real-world complexities into abstract models that can be systematically studied.

The primary objective of mathematical modeling is not merely to obtain numerical solutions, but to gain qualitative understanding of system behavior, identify key parame-ters, and explore possible future scenarios. In the modern era, mathematical models play a crucial role in policymaking, environmental management, public health planning, and sustainable development.

1.2 Historical Background

The origins of mathematical modeling can be traced back to classical mechanics, where Newtonian laws were used to describe physical motion. In the eighteenth century, Thomas Malthus introduced one of the earliest population growth models, highlighting the appli-cation of mathematics to social phenomena. Later, Pierre-Francois Verhulst refined this idea through the logistic growth model.

In the natural sciences, Lotka and Volterra independently developed predator–prey models in the early twentieth century, laying the foundation for mathematical ecology.

The second half of the twentieth century witnessed rapid growth in systems theory, non- linear dynamics, and computational modeling, enabling the study of highly complex social and environmental systems.

1.3 Basic Concepts and Definitions

1.3.1 System

A system is a collection of interacting components that together exhibit behavior not evident from the individual parts alone.

1.3.2 Mathematical Model

A mathematical model is a simplified representation of a real-world system using mathematical variables, parameters, equations, and logical relationships.

1.3.3 State Variables and Parameters

State variables describe the evolving condition of the system, while parameters represent fixed quantities influencing system behavior.

1.3.4 Deterministic and Stochastic Models

- Deterministic models produce the same output for given initial conditions.
- Stochastic models incorporate randomness to account for uncertainty and vari-ability.

1.4 General Steps in Mathematical Modeling

The process of mathematical modeling typically involves the following steps:

1. Identification of the problem and objectives
2. Selection of relevant variables and parameters
3. Formulation of mathematical relationships
4. Analysis and solution of the model
5. Validation using empirical data

6. Interpretation and refinement

1.5 Population Growth Models

1.5.1 Exponential Growth Model

The simplest population growth model assumes unlimited resources:

dP

= rP (1.1)

dt

where P (t) is the population at time t and r is the intrinsic growth rate. The solution is given by:

P (t) = P0ert (1.2)

1.5.2 Logistic Growth Model

To account for limited resources, the logistic model is used:

dP = rP 1 − P (1.3)

dt

where K is the carrying capacity of the environment.

1.6 Modeling Social Systems

1.6.1 Opinion Dynamics Models

Social opinion formation can be modeled using averaging processes. One simple discrete- time model is:

n

xi (t + 1) = wijxj(t) (1.4)

j=1

where xi(t) represents the opinion of individual i at time t and wij denotes the influence weight.

1.6.2 Epidemic Models

The spread of infectious diseases is a classical example of social-nature interaction.

SIR Model

The SIR model divides the population into three compartments:

- $S(t)$: Susceptible individuals
- $I(t)$: Infected individuals
- $R(t)$: Recovered individuals The governing equations are:

dtdtdt

where β is the transmission rate and γ is the recovery rate.

1.7 Modeling Natural Systems

1.7.1 Predator–Prey Model

The Lotka–Volterra model describes interactions between predator and prey species:

$$\frac{dx}{dt} = ax - bxy \qquad (1.8)$$

$$\frac{dy}{dt} = -cy + dxy \qquad (1.9)$$

where $x(t)$ is the prey population and $y(t)$ is the predator population.

1.7.2 Environmental Resource Models

Renewable resources such as forests and fisheries can be modeled using harvesting equa-tions:

$$\frac{dR}{dt} = f(R) - H \qquad (1.10)$$

where R represents the resource stock and H is the harvesting rate.

1.8 Case Study: Urban Population and Resource Stress

Consider an urban region experiencing rapid population growth. Let P (t) denote the population and W (t) the water demand. A coupled model can be written as:

1.9. Figures and Illustrations

$$\frac{dP}{dt} = rP \qquad 1 - P \qquad (1.11)$$

$$W(t) = \alpha P(t) \qquad (1.12)$$

Such models assist planners in predicting future resource requirements and infrastruc-ture needs.

1.9 Figures and Illustrations

Population Growth Curve

Figure 1.1: Exponential and Logistic Population Growth

Predator–Prey Phase Diagram

Figure 1.2: Dynamics of Predator–Prey Interaction

1.10 Advantages and Limitations of Mathematical Models

1.10.1 Advantages

- Provide quantitative insights
- Aid in prediction and scenario analysis
- Support decision-making and policy formulation

1.10.2 Limitations

- Dependence on assumptions
- Sensitivity to parameter estimation
- Difficulty in capturing human behavior accurately

1.11 Modern Trends and Developments

Recent advances include agent-based modeling, network-based models, and data-driven approaches using machine learning. These techniques allow more realistic representation of heterogeneous agents and complex interactions in social and natural systems.

1.12 Conclusion

Mathematical modeling serves as a bridge between abstract theory and real-world ap-plications. By systematically translating social and natural phenomena into mathemat-ical language, models enable deeper understanding, prediction, and informed decision- making. Despite inherent limitations, mathematical models remain indispensable tools in addressing contemporary global challenges such as population growth, epidemics, and environmental sustainability.

Chapter 7

Legal Frameworks for Environmental and Agriculture Sustainability

Dr. Vidya Shaktawat
Professor, Faculty of Law, Madhav University, Pindwara, Sirohi

7.1 Introduction: Law as the Architecture of Sustainable Living

Sustainable living has emerged in the twenty-first century as both a moral imperative and a structural necessity. It represents a conscious reorientation of human development toward ecological balance, social justice, and economic resilience. While sustainability is often framed in environmental or technological terms, its realization ultimately depends upon normative systems that regulate conduct, allocate resources, and resolve conflicts. Law, in this context, functions as the architecture of sustainable living. It provides the institutional design through which societies translate ecological awareness into enforceable standards, collective responsibilities, and long-term policy commitments. Without a robust legal framework, sustainability remains an inspirational slogan; with it, sustainability becomes an operational principle embedded in governance. The intellectual foundation of sustainable living rests upon the idea of intergenerational equity the obligation of present generations to preserve natural and social resources for future generations. This ethical premise gained global recognition in the late twentieth century, especially after the articulation of sustainable development as development that meets present needs without compromising future capacities. However, ethical aspirations alone cannot secure ecological integrity. Societies require mechanisms to define limits, regulate exploitation, ensure accountability, and harmonize competing interests. Law performs precisely these functions. By codifying environmental standards, establishing property regimes, regulating agricultural practices, and creating institutional oversight, legal systems transform moral commitments into enforceable obligations.

Environmental sustainability and agricultural sustainability are deeply interconnected. Agriculture depends upon soil fertility, water availability, climatic stability and biodiversity—all of which are shaped by environmental governance. At the same time, agricultural practices influence environmental outcomes through land use changes, chemical inputs, irrigation systems, and livestock management. Thus, sustainable living requires an integrated legal approach that addresses both environmental protection and agricultural regulation in a unified framework. Fragmented legal regimes, where environmental laws operate separately from agricultural policies, often generate contradictions that undermine sustainability objectives. Law must therefore function as a coordinating architecture, aligning sectoral policies within a coherent ecological vision. In the Indian legal context, the evolution of sustainability has been profoundly influenced by constitutional interpretation. Although the Constitution does not explicitly employ the terminology of "sustainable development," its values reflect a deep concern for social welfare, equitable resource distribution, and environmental protection.

Judicial interpretation of the right to life has expanded its scope to include the right to a clean and healthy environment, thereby elevating ecological protection to a fundamental constitutional concern. This jurisprudential development illustrates how law adapts to emerging societal challenges and incorporates environmental ethics into the core of constitutional governance. Beyond constitutional interpretation, legislative enactments form the structural pillars of sustainable living. Statutes regulating pollution control, forest conservation, biodiversity protection, and environmental impact assessment create regulatory boundaries for economic activity. Agricultural laws governing land tenure, seed certification, fertilizer use, and water management shape patterns of cultivation and resource consumption. These legal instruments do more than control harm; they also incentivize sustainable practices, promote innovation, and protect vulnerable communities. By structuring incentives and disincentives, law guides behavior toward ecological responsibility.

Law also plays a redistributive role in sustainability. Environmental degradation disproportionately affects marginalized populations—small farmers, indigenous communities, and urban poor residents. Unsustainable agricultural policies may intensify inequality by favoring capital-intensive practices over traditional knowledge systems. Legal frameworks can correct such imbalances by recognizing community rights over forests, ensuring access to water resources, protecting farmers' seed sovereignty, and facilitating participatory governance. In doing so, law bridges the gap between environmental protection and social justice, reinforcing the holistic character of sustainable living. Another critical dimension of law as architectural framework lies in its preventive function. Environmental harm often manifests irreversibly, making post-facto remedies inadequate. Legal principles such as the precautionary approach require authorities to anticipate potential ecological risks and adopt preventive measures even in the absence of complete scientific certainty. This shift from reactive to proactive governance reflects the maturation of environmental jurisprudence. Sustainable living demands foresight and law institutionalizes that foresight through regulatory planning, environmental clearances, and risk assessment procedures. Moreover, law provides mechanisms of accountability that are indispensable for sustainability. Regulatory agencies monitor compliance with environmental standards; courts adjudicate disputes and impose liabilities; administrative bodies conduct inspections and issue sanctions. The polluter pays principle, widely recognized in environmental jurisprudence, ensures that those responsible for environmental damage bear the cost of restoration. Such accountability mechanisms deter harmful practices and internalize environmental costs within economic decision-making. By embedding ecological considerations within market systems, law fosters a more sustainable economic order.

The role of law extends beyond regulation into the realm of governance design. Institutions such as environmental tribunals, biodiversity authorities, and agricultural research councils operate within legal mandates that define their powers and responsibilities. Decentralized governance structures, including local self-government institutions, enable community participation in resource management. Sustainable living cannot be imposed solely through centralized authority; it requires inclusive decision-making processes that reflect local realities and indigenous knowledge. Law facilitates this inclusivity by recognizing participatory rights and procedural fairness in environmental decision-making.

Globalization further complicates the architecture of sustainability. Environmental challenges such as climate change, biodiversity loss, and transboundary pollution transcend national boundaries. International agreements and multilateral environmental treaties influence domestic legislation and policy choices. Trade regimes affect agricultural subsidies, food standards, and intellectual property rights related to seeds and biotechnology. Consequently, national legal systems must navigate complex intersections between domestic priorities and international commitments. Law serves as the interface between global norms and local implementation, ensuring that sustainability objectives align with both national sovereignty and global responsibility.

Technological advancement presents both opportunities and regulatory dilemmas within the sustainability framework. Innovations such as precision agriculture, genetically modified crops, renewable energy systems, and digital monitoring tools offer potential solutions to resource scarcity and environmental degradation. However, they also raise concerns regarding bio safety, data privacy, ecological risk, and equitable access. Legal frameworks must adapt to these emerging realities by balancing innovation with precaution, ensuring that technological progress contributes to sustainability rather than undermines it. In this sense, law is not static architecture but a dynamic design that evolves in response to changing social and scientific contexts.

An important feature of sustainable living is its integrative character. Environmental protection, agricultural productivity, public health, economic development, and social equity are interdependent components of a single systemic whole. Law must therefore transcend compartmentalized approaches and embrace integrative governance models. For instance, water regulation must consider agricultural irrigation needs, ecosystem preservation, and urban consumption patterns simultaneously. Land use planning must reconcile industrial expansion with food security and forest conservation. Such integrated policymaking requires harmonization of statutes, coordination among ministries, and coherent judicial interpretation. Law, as the architecture of sustainability, provides the blueprint for such harmonization. Despite its centrality, law alone cannot guarantee sustainable living. Implementation challenges, administrative inefficiencies, political pressures, and socio-economic inequalities may dilute the transformative potential of legal frameworks. However, these limitations do not diminish the foundational importance of law; rather, they highlight the need for stronger institutions, public awareness, and participatory engagement. Sustainable living is a collective endeavor, and law establishes the structural conditions within which this collective effort can flourish.

The normative dimension of law also deserves attention. Legal systems embody societal values and priorities. When sustainability becomes embedded within constitutional principles, statutory mandates, and judicial doctrines, it signals a shift in collective consciousness. Law thus performs an educative function, shaping public attitudes toward environmental stewardship and responsible agriculture. Through curriculum reforms, awareness campaigns, and rights-based litigation, legal processes cultivate ecological citizenship. In this way, law does not merely regulate behavior; it nurtures a culture of sustainability.

In contemporary discourse, sustainable living increasingly intersects with human rights. Access to clean water, nutritious food, safe housing, and a healthy environment are recognized as essential components of dignified life. Agricultural sustainability ensures food security and rural livelihoods, while environmental sustainability safeguards health and ecological resilience. Legal recognition of these interconnected rights strengthens the moral and institutional basis of sustainable living. Courts have acknowledged that environmental degradation undermines fundamental rights, thereby reinforcing the constitutional legitimacy of sustainability measures. Furthermore, sustainable living demands long-term vision beyond electoral cycles and short-term economic gains. Law contributes stability and continuity through codified standards and institutional memory. Legislative enactments endure beyond political transitions, providing consistent policy direction. Judicial precedents guide administrative discretion and ensure uniform application of principles. This continuity is crucial for addressing environmental challenges that unfold over decades, such as climate change and soil degradation. Law, therefore, functions as a temporal bridge connecting present action with future consequences.

In the agricultural sector, sustainability requires balancing productivity with ecological sensitivity. Legal frameworks can encourage crop diversification, organic farming, integrated pest management, and conservation agriculture. They can regulate groundwater extraction, promote rainwater harvesting, and incentivize renewable energy use in irrigation. By structuring subsidies and market incentives in favor of sustainable practices, law aligns economic rationality with ecological prudence. Such alignment transforms sustainability from a cost burden into a strategic advantage.

The architecture of sustainable living ultimately rests upon coherence—coherence between rights and duties, development and conservation, local autonomy and national policy, innovation and precaution. Law provides the structural coherence necessary to integrate these dimensions. It defines the contours of permissible activity, mediates conflicts between competing interests, and establishes forums for dialogue and redress. Through legislation, adjudication, and administration, law constructs the institutional scaffolding of sustainability. In conclusion, sustainable living is not an accidental outcome of technological progress or voluntary goodwill; it is the product of deliberate legal design. Law acts as the architect, drafting blueprints that organize human interaction with nature and among communities. In the Indian context, constitutional values, statutory enactments, and judicial doctrines collectively form this architecture. Yet, sustainability remains an evolving project, requiring continuous refinement of legal frameworks in response to environmental realities and social aspirations. By embedding ecological ethics within the rule of law, societies can transform sustainability from a peripheral concern into a central organizing principle of governance. Through such legal architecture, sustainable living becomes not only possible but institutionally secure, ensuring harmony between humanity and the natural world for generations to come.

7.2 Constitutional Foundations of Environmental and Agricultural Sustainability

The constitutional framework of India provides the normative and structural foundation upon which environmental and agricultural sustainability is built. Although the Constitution does not explicitly employ the expression "sustainable development," its text, spirit, and judicial interpretation collectively embody principles that align closely with ecological balance, social equity, and responsible governance. The Constitution serves not merely as a political charter but as a transformative document that guides the State in harmonizing development with environmental protection and agricultural welfare. Sustainability, therefore, derives its legitimacy and enforceability from constitutional values that prioritize human dignity, distributive justice, and intergenerational responsibility. At the heart of constitutional environmentalism lies Article 21, which guarantees the right to life and personal liberty. Over time, the judiciary has expansively interpreted this provision to include the right to live in a clean and healthy environment. The Supreme Court has consistently affirmed that life under Article 21 is not confined to mere animal existence but encompasses the right to live with human dignity, health, and ecological security. By recognizing environmental quality as integral to the right to life, the Court effectively constitutionalized environmental protection. This interpretation has enabled citizens to seek judicial remedies against pollution, deforestation, and ecological degradation, thereby transforming environmental protection from a policy aspiration into a fundamental right.

The Directive Principles of State Policy further reinforce the constitutional commitment to sustainability. Article 48A directs the State to protect and improve the environment and safeguard forests and wildlife. Although Directive Principles are not enforceable in courts, they serve as guiding principles for legislative and executive action. They articulate the moral and developmental vision of the Constitution, encouraging policies that prioritize ecological conservation and sustainable resource management. Article 47, which emphasizes the duty of the State to improve public health and raise the level of nutrition, indirectly connects environmental protection with agricultural sustainability. Clean water, fertile soil, and pollution-free air are indispensable to public health and food security. Thus, environmental governance and agricultural policy are constitutionally intertwined through the objective of ensuring human well-being.

Article 39(b) of the Directive Principles advocates that ownership and control of material resources of the community should be so distributed as to subserve the common good. This provision has profound implications for land, water, forests, and agricultural inputs. Sustainable agriculture depends upon equitable access to productive resources, prevention of over-exploitation, and responsible stewardship. By mandating distributive justice, the Constitution underscores that natural resources are not commodities for unrestrained private exploitation but assets to be managed for collective benefit. This principle resonates with contemporary sustainability discourse, which emphasizes the need to balance economic growth with social equity and ecological limits.

Complementing these provisions are the Fundamental Duties enumerated under Article 51A(g), which impose upon every citizen the duty to protect and improve the natural environment, including forests, lakes, rivers, and wildlife. Although not directly enforceable, Fundamental Duties play an important normative role in shaping civic consciousness and influencing judicial interpretation. Courts have often invoked Article 51A(g) to justify environmental restrictions and encourage participatory governance. By embedding environmental responsibility within the framework of citizenship, the Constitution promotes a culture of shared stewardship rather than exclusive reliance on State action. Sustainable living thus emerges as a collaborative endeavor grounded in constitutional ethics.

Agricultural sustainability also intersects significantly with the federal structure of the Constitution. Under the Seventh Schedule, agriculture, land, irrigation, and fisheries fall primarily within the State List, granting States legislative competence in these areas. Environmental protection, however, is addressed through entries in the Concurrent List, enabling both Union and State governments to legislate. This distribution of powers necessitates cooperative federalism in implementing sustainability measures. For instance, groundwater regulation, forest conservation, biodiversity management, and climate adaptation strategies require coordinated action between central and state authorities. The constitutional design accommodates regional diversity in agricultural practices while ensuring national standards for environmental protection.

The constitutional scheme thus establishes a tripartite model for sustainability governance: enforceable fundamental rights, directive principles guiding public policy, and civic duties fostering environmental responsibility. This model ensures that sustainability is not confined to executive discretion but anchored in constitutional legitimacy. Judicial review further strengthens this architecture by holding governmental actions accountable to constitutional mandates. Courts have not hesitated to invalidate projects or policies that threaten ecological balance or violate environmental rights. In essence, the Constitution of India operates as a living instrument capable of responding to emerging ecological challenges. Its provisions create a normative environment in which environmental protection and agricultural sustainability are not peripheral concerns but integral components of governance. By embedding sustainability within the constitutional framework, India has laid a strong foundation for integrating development with ecological prudence. The challenge lies in translating these constitutional ideals into consistent legislative action and effective implementation, ensuring that the promise of sustainability becomes a tangible reality for present and future generations.

7.3 Evolution of Environmental Legislation in India

The evolution of environmental legislation in India reflects the nation's gradual recognition of ecological protection as an essential component of governance and development. In the early decades following independence, legislative attention was primarily directed toward economic growth, industrial expansion, and agricultural modernization. Environmental concerns, though present in scattered statutory provisions, did not constitute a unified policy objective. Laws such as the Indian Forest Act, 1927, and the Factories Act, 1948, addressed specific regulatory needs forest administration and industrial safety respectively but lacked a comprehensive environmental philosophy. These enactments were primarily resource-management or labor-oriented statutes rather than instruments of ecological sustainability. The transformation of environmental law in India began in earnest during the 1970s, catalyzed by global environmental awareness and domestic ecological challenges. The 1972 United Nations Conference on the Human Environment in Stockholm marked a watershed moment. India's participation in the conference underscored its commitment to integrating environmental considerations into national policy. In the years that followed, legislative reforms signaled a decisive shift toward structured environmental governance.

The Water (Prevention and Control of Pollution) Act, 1974, was among the earliest comprehensive environmental statutes enacted in the post-Stockholm era. It established Central and State Pollution Control Boards tasked with preventing and controlling water pollution. The Act empowered authorities to set effluent standards, inspect industrial facilities, and take enforcement action against violators. By institutionalizing regulatory oversight, it marked the beginning of a systematic approach to pollution control. The creation of regulatory bodies signified recognition that environmental protection required specialized institutions and continuous monitoring rather than sporadic intervention. Building upon this framework, the Air (Prevention and Control of Pollution) Act, 1981, extended regulatory mechanisms to air quality management. Industrial emissions, vehicular pollution, and urbanization had begun to degrade air quality in major cities, posing serious public health risks. The Air Act reinforced the authority of Pollution Control Boards and introduced standards for emission control. Together, the Water and Air Acts laid the groundwork for a coordinated pollution control regime, emphasizing compliance, licensing, and penal consequences for environmental violations.

A major turning point in Indian environmental legislation occurred in the aftermath of the Bhopal Gas Tragedy of 1984, one of the most devastating industrial disasters in history. The tragedy exposed significant gaps in industrial regulation and emergency preparedness. In response, Parliament enacted the Environment (Protection) Act, 1986. This statute provided a broad, umbrella framework empowering the central government to take measures for protecting and improving environmental quality. It authorized the issuance of notifications regulating hazardous substances, environmental impact assessments, and standards for emissions and discharges. The Act's wide-ranging powers enabled the government to address emerging environmental challenges with flexibility and speed.

Parallel to pollution control legislation, laws aimed at conserving natural ecosystems gained prominence. The Wildlife (Protection) Act, 1972, sought to preserve biodiversity by regulating hunting, protecting endangered species, and establishing protected areas such as national parks and wildlife sanctuaries. The Forest (Conservation) Act, 1980, restricted the diversion of forest land for non-forest purposes without central approval, thereby curbing deforestation and preserving ecological balance. These statutes recognized that forests and wildlife are not merely economic resources but ecological assets essential for climate stability, water conservation and agricultural productivity. In the early twenty-first century, environmental legislation expanded to incorporate principles of equity and community participation. The Biological Diversity Act, 2002, was enacted to fulfill India's obligations under international biodiversity agreements. It aimed to conserve biological resources, regulate access to genetic material, and ensure fair and equitable sharing of benefits arising from their use. By recognizing the role of local communities and traditional knowledge, the Act integrated conservation with social justice, reinforcing the holistic approach to sustainability.

Despite the breadth of legislative measures, environmental law in India has often been criticized for being reactive rather than preventive. Many statutes emerged in response to crises industrial disasters, deforestation, or international commitments rather than as part of a proactive environmental strategy. Enforcement remains a persistent challenge. Pollution Control Boards frequently face resource constraints, technical limitations and administrative pressures. Environmental clearance processes have sometimes been perceived as procedural formalities rather than rigorous assessments of ecological impact. Economic growth imperatives occasionally overshadow environmental considerations, leading to tensions between development and conservation. Nevertheless, the legislative architecture constructed over the past five decades provides a substantial foundation for sustainable governance. It establishes regulatory standards, institutional mechanisms, and enforcement procedures that collectively shape environmental management. The integration of environmental impact assessments, public hearings, and compliance monitoring reflects a maturing legal system responsive to ecological concerns. Furthermore, judicial interpretation has reinforced legislative intent by expanding environmental rights and strengthening accountability.

The evolution of environmental legislation in India thus represents a gradual but significant shift from fragmented resource management to an integrated framework of environmental protection. While challenges of implementation and coherence persist, the statutory regime has laid the groundwork for aligning environmental governance with agricultural sustainability and broader developmental objectives. As ecological pressures intensify in the era of climate change and resource scarcity, the continued refinement and effective enforcement of environmental laws will remain central to India's pursuit of sustainable living.

7.4 Sustainable Development as a Judicial Doctrine

The doctrine of sustainable development in India has largely evolved through judicial interpretation rather than explicit legislative articulation. Indian environmental jurisprudence demonstrates how courts, particularly the Supreme Court and various High Courts, have transformed constitutional principles into actionable standards of ecological governance. In the absence of a detailed statutory definition of sustainable development, the judiciary has played a pioneering role in harmonizing environmental protection with economic progress, thereby embedding sustainability within the framework of constitutional law.

The courts have consistently emphasized that development cannot proceed at the cost of irreversible environmental degradation. By interpreting the right to life under Article 21 as encompassing the right to a healthy environment, the judiciary has established that ecological balance is integral to human dignity and well-being. In this interpretative process, the principle of sustainable development has emerged as a guiding norm requiring the State to strike a balance between developmental aspirations and environmental preservation. Judicial pronouncements have clarified that neither development nor conservation can claim absolute priority; instead, a rational equilibrium must be maintained.

Three foundational principles have shaped the judicial articulation of sustainable development in India: the precautionary principle, the polluter pays principle, and the public trust doctrine. The precautionary principle mandates that authorities must anticipate, prevent, and mitigate environmental harm even when scientific evidence is uncertain. This shifts the burden of proof onto those proposing potentially harmful activities, reinforcing preventive governance. The polluter pays principle ensures that individuals or industries responsible for environmental damage bear the financial cost of remediation, internalizing environmental costs within economic decision-making. The public trust doctrine recognizes natural resources such as forests, rivers, and coastal areas as assets held by the State in trust for present and future generations, limiting arbitrary or exploitative allocation.

Public Interest Litigation (PIL) has served as a crucial procedural innovation in advancing environmental justice. By relaxing rules of locus standi, the judiciary has empowered citizens, environmental groups, and social activists to approach courts on behalf of affected communities and ecological interests. PIL has facilitated judicial scrutiny of illegal mining operations, industrial pollution, deforestation, and unsustainable infrastructure projects. Through continuing mandamus and monitoring mechanisms, courts have directed the formulation of environmental impact assessments, closure of hazardous industries, and restoration of degraded ecosystems. While judicial activism in environmental matters has been instrumental in strengthening sustainability norms, it has also prompted debates regarding separation of powers and the proper limits of judicial intervention. Critics argue that courts sometimes enter the domain of policy formulation, traditionally reserved for the executive and legislature. Nevertheless, the judiciary's proactive stance has filled regulatory gaps and reinforced constitutional commitments to environmental protection. In doing so, it has transformed sustainable development from a policy objective into a binding judicial doctrine that continues to shape India's environmental governance.

7.5 Legal Regulation of Agricultural Sustainability

Agricultural sustainability represents a multidimensional objective that integrates ecological integrity with economic viability and social equity. It encompasses soil conservation, efficient water management, crop diversification, biodiversity preservation, seed security, and climate resilience. In India, the legal regulation of agriculture operates through a mosaic of statutes, subordinate legislation, and policy instruments that collectively influence farming practices and rural development. Although agriculture is primarily a State subject under the constitutional scheme, both Union and State laws significantly shape the contours of sustainable agricultural governance.

Historically, land reform laws were enacted to prevent concentration of landholdings, abolish intermediaries, and promote equitable distribution of agricultural land. These reforms sought to advance social justice and enhance productivity. However, persistent challenges such as land fragmentation, insecure tenancy arrangements, and declining soil quality continue to impede sustainable land use. Contemporary agricultural sustainability requires a renewed legal focus on consolidation of holdings, secure land tenure, and incentives for conservation-oriented practices. Legal recognition of agro ecology, organic farming, and regenerative agriculture is gradually gaining importance, reflecting a shift from purely productivity-driven models toward environmentally sensitive cultivation. Seed regulation constitutes a crucial pillar of agricultural sustainability. The Seeds Act, 1966, introduced mechanisms for quality control, certification, and regulation of seed distribution to ensure reliability and crop performance. Subsequently, the Protection of Plant Varieties and Farmers' Rights Act, 2001, established a balanced framework that protects breeders' intellectual property rights while safeguarding farmers' traditional practices. By recognizing farmers as cultivators, conservers, and breeders of plant varieties, the law affirms their contribution to biodiversity conservation and seed sovereignty. This dual protection model supports innovation without undermining indigenous knowledge systems.

Chemical input regulation also plays a vital role in sustainable agriculture. The Fertilizer Control Order and the Insecticides Act regulate the manufacture, sale, and use of fertilizers and pesticides. While these laws were initially framed to ensure product quality and prevent misuse, contemporary concerns about soil degradation, groundwater contamination, and ecological toxicity have prompted calls for stricter oversight. Increasing emphasis is being placed on integrated nutrient management, promotion of bio-fertilizers, organic inputs, and environmentally friendly pest control methods. Legal reform in this area aims to reduce dependency on chemical-intensive farming and encourage balanced agricultural ecosystems.

Food security legislation further intersects with agricultural sustainability. The National Food Security Act, 2013, seeks to ensure access to adequate food through public distribution mechanisms and nutritional support programs. Although primarily welfare-oriented, it indirectly shapes agricultural production patterns by influencing procurement policies and crop selection. However, long-term sustainability demands a transition from quantity-centric approaches toward quality-focused, climate-resilient, and ecologically responsible agricultural systems.

In essence, the legal regulation of agricultural sustainability in India reflects an evolving framework that balances productivity, environmental protection, and farmers' rights. Strengthening enforcement, promoting sustainable incentives, and harmonizing agricultural laws with environmental objectives remain essential for achieving holistic and enduring sustainability.

7.6 Climate Change and Agricultural Law

Climate change has emerged as one of the most significant challenges confronting agricultural sustainability in the twenty-first century. Rising temperatures, unpredictable rainfall patterns, prolonged droughts, floods, and extreme weather events directly threaten crop productivity, soil health, water availability, and rural livelihoods. Agriculture, being both a contributor to and a victim of climate change, requires a carefully structured legal response that integrates mitigation and adaptation strategies. In this context, climate change law and agricultural regulation must function in a coordinated and mutually reinforcing manner.

India's climate governance framework is primarily policy-driven, with the National Action Plan on Climate Change (NAPCC) serving as a central guiding document. The NAPCC outlines missions on sustainable agriculture, water conservation, renewable energy, and climate resilience. The National Mission for Sustainable Agriculture specifically focuses on climate-resilient crops, soil health management, efficient irrigation, and risk management. However, as these initiatives largely operate through executive policies and schemes, there is an increasing need for statutory reinforcement to ensure continuity, accountability, and enforceability. Comprehensive climate change legislation could provide clearer mandates, institutional responsibilities, and monitoring mechanisms.

Legal intersections between climate regulation and agriculture are evident in several domains. Carbon mitigation efforts, including promotion of renewable energy and reduction of greenhouse gas emissions, directly influence agricultural practices. Incentives for solar-powered irrigation systems, energy-efficient equipment, and sustainable land use contribute to both environmental protection and farm resilience. Similarly, laws governing afforestation, land restoration and conservation agriculture support carbon sequestration and ecosystem stability.

The Disaster Management Act, 2005, provides an institutional framework to address climate-induced disasters such as floods, droughts, cyclones, and heat waves. By establishing national and state disaster management authorities, the Act facilitates coordinated response, preparedness planning, and relief measures. Although not exclusively climate-focused, its mechanisms are crucial in safeguarding agricultural communities from climate shocks. Complementing this framework are crop insurance schemes and risk mitigation programs designed to protect farmers against crop failure. While policy-based, these schemes operate within regulatory guidelines that aim to provide financial stability and reduce vulnerability.

Climate-smart agriculture requires harmonization of environmental statutes with agricultural planning. Water conservation laws, groundwater regulation measures, and watershed development programs must align with climate adaptation goals. Unsustainable groundwater extraction, for instance, exacerbates climate vulnerability and undermines long-term productivity. Legal instruments must therefore encourage efficient irrigation, rainwater harvesting, and ecosystem-based adaptation strategies. Furthermore, climate change law must incorporate principles of climate justice. Small and marginal farmers, indigenous communities, and rural laborers often bear the brunt of environmental disruptions despite contributing minimally to greenhouse gas emissions. Legal frameworks should prioritize their protection through equitable resource allocation, access to adaptation technologies, and participatory decision-making. In this way, climate change and agricultural law together form a critical component of sustainable living, ensuring resilience, equity, and ecological balance in an era of environmental uncertainty.

7.7 International Environmental and Agricultural Law

International environmental and agricultural law plays a decisive role in shaping domestic sustainability frameworks, particularly in countries navigating the dual imperatives of development and ecological protection. In an era of globalization, environmental degradation, climate change, biodiversity loss, and food insecurity transcend national boundaries, necessitating coordinated global responses. Multilateral agreements such as the Paris Agreement, the Convention on Biological

Diversity (CBD), and the United Nations Framework Convention on Climate Change (UNFCCC) establish normative standards and cooperative mechanisms that influence national legislation and policy formulation. Even where commitments are non-binding, they generate persuasive obligations that guide domestic environmental governance and agricultural planning. For a country like India, participation in these international regimes requires harmonization of domestic laws with global sustainability objectives. Climate mitigation targets, biodiversity conservation strategies, and adaptation measures are often incorporated into national action plans and sectoral policies. This alignment reflects the growing interdependence between international commitments and internal regulatory frameworks.

Trade law further complicates this relationship. Agreements under the World Trade Organization (WTO) regulate agricultural subsidies, sanitary and phytosanitary measures, and intellectual property rights relating to seeds and biotechnology. While such rules promote market access and economic integration, they may constrain policy space for supporting small farmers or implementing protective environmental standards. Balancing trade competitiveness with ecological sustainability and food sovereignty remains a complex legal challenge.

The principle of common but differentiated responsibilities (CBDR) is particularly significant in this context. It acknowledges that developed and developing countries bear different historical responsibilities and capacities in addressing environmental problems. For developing nations, international environmental law must accommodate developmental priorities while ensuring progressive ecological stewardship. Issues such as transboundary water management, equitable access to genetic resources, and climate finance highlight the intricate connection between global norms and local sustainability goals. Thus, international environmental and agricultural law forms an essential dimension of holistic sustainable living, reinforcing the need for cooperative yet equitable global governance.

7.8 Governance Mechanisms and Institutional Frameworks

The effectiveness of legal frameworks for environmental and agricultural sustainability ultimately depends upon the strength, coordination, and accountability of institutional mechanisms. Laws, however progressive in design, require competent authorities and functional governance structures for meaningful implementation. In India, a network of regulatory and adjudicatory bodies operates at national, state, and local levels to enforce environmental standards and promote sustainable agricultural practices. Pollution Control Boards are entrusted with monitoring emissions, granting consents, and initiating action against violators. Biodiversity Authorities oversee conservation efforts and regulate access to biological resources, while Agricultural Departments design and implement schemes related to soil health, irrigation, crop diversification, and farmer welfare.

A significant institutional innovation in environmental governance has been the establishment of the National Green Tribunal (NGT). The NGT provides specialized adjudication of environmental disputes, ensuring expeditious resolution and technical expertise in complex ecological matters. By offering an accessible forum for environmental grievances, it strengthens accountability and enhances access to environmental justice. Its decisions often reinforce principles such as precaution, restoration, and sustainable development, thereby supporting the broader sustainability framework.

Decentralized governance mechanisms also play a vital role. Panchayati Raj institutions and urban local bodies facilitate community-based resource management and participatory decision-making. Local self-governments are uniquely positioned to regulate water usage, encourage organic farming initiatives, implement watershed development programs, and monitor compliance with environmental norms. Such grassroots engagement ensures that sustainability is rooted in local realities and collective responsibility rather than imposed solely through centralized authority. Despite this institutional architecture, challenges persist. Overlapping jurisdictions, inadequate funding, limited technical expertise, and bureaucratic delays frequently undermine effective enforcement. Coordination between environmental and agricultural departments is often fragmented, resulting in policy inconsistencies. Strengthening institutional capacity through training, digital governance tools, transparency mechanisms, and inter-agency collaboration is therefore essential. A well-integrated and responsive governance framework remains the cornerstone of translating sustainability laws into tangible environmental and agricultural outcomes.

7.9 Emerging Trends: Technology, Innovation, and Legal Reform

Technological advancement is rapidly transforming the landscape of environmental governance and agricultural sustainability. Innovations such as precision farming, satellite-based monitoring systems, artificial intelligence-driven crop analysis, and blockchain-enabled supply chain management are enhancing efficiency, transparency, and resource optimization. Precision agriculture, for instance, allows farmers to apply water, fertilizers, and pesticides in measured quantities based on real-time data, thereby reducing waste and environmental harm. Satellite and remote sensing technologies assist in monitoring deforestation, soil health, and water usage, strengthening regulatory compliance. However, these developments also raise new legal questions concerning data ownership, digital access, cyber security, and equitable distribution of technological benefits. Legal frameworks must evolve to regulate digital agriculture while ensuring that small and marginal farmers are not excluded from technological progress.

Biotechnology represents another significant frontier in sustainability discourse. Genetically modified organisms (GMOs) promise higher yields, pest resistance, and climate resilience, yet they also generate concerns regarding biosafety, ecological imbalance, and long-term health implications. Regulatory regimes must strike a careful balance between promoting scientific innovation and upholding precautionary safeguards. Transparent approval processes, environmental risk assessments, and liability mechanisms are essential components of responsible biotechnology governance.

The integration of renewable energy into agriculture further exemplifies the intersection of innovation and sustainability law. Solar-powered irrigation systems, bioenergy initiatives, and decentralized renewable grids reduce dependence on fossil fuels while enhancing farm resilience. Supportive policies, financial incentives, and regulatory clarity are necessary to mainstream such technologies within agricultural systems. Increasingly, sustainability law is becoming interdisciplinary, drawing upon environmental science, economics, public health, and social justice. Future legal reforms must embrace holistic governance models that link agriculture, environmental protection, trade regulation, and health policy in a coherent framework. By adapting to technological change while safeguarding ecological and social interests, legal systems can ensure that innovation contributes meaningfully to sustainable living rather than exacerbating inequality or environmental risk.

7.10 Challenges in Implementation

While India possesses an extensive body of environmental and agricultural legislation, the true test of sustainability lies in effective implementation. Progressive statutory frameworks often falter at the stage of execution due to fragmented policies, overlapping jurisdictions, and administrative inefficiencies. Coordination gaps between environmental authorities, agricultural departments, and local governance institutions weaken the coherence necessary for integrated sustainability. Bureaucratic inertia, procedural delays, and inadequate monitoring mechanisms further reduce the impact of well-intentioned laws. In some instances, political pressures and economic considerations influence environmental clearances or dilute regulatory standards, thereby compromising ecological integrity in favor of short-term development goals. Corruption and lack of transparency also undermine regulatory enforcement. Environmental impact assessments may be treated as procedural formalities rather than rigorous scientific evaluations. Similarly, agricultural reforms intended to promote soil conservation or water efficiency may remain underutilized due to weak supervision and accountability deficits. Strengthening institutional oversight and ensuring transparent decision-making processes are therefore critical to bridging the gap between law and practice.

A significant challenge arises from limited awareness among farmers and rural communities regarding sustainability schemes and legal entitlements. Without adequate legal literacy and extension services, farmers may be unable to access benefits related to organic certification, crop insurance, water conservation programs, or biodiversity protection. Participatory planning and community engagement are essential to ensure that sustainability initiatives reflect local needs and knowledge systems. Moreover, sustainability requires long-term political commitment and societal transformation. Balancing economic growth with ecological limits often involves difficult trade-offs that demand visionary leadership. Legal provisions alone cannot alter entrenched agricultural practices unless accompanied by economic incentives, capacity-building programs, and public awareness campaigns. Behavioral change, cultural adaptation and collective responsibility are indispensable components of sustainable living. Consequently, legal frameworks must function in synergy with policy innovation, institutional reform, and social mobilization to achieve meaningful and lasting sustainability outcomes.

7.11 Toward an Integrated Legal Framework for Sustainable Living

Achieving sustainable living requires a decisive movement away from fragmented regulatory approaches toward a unified and integrated legal framework. Environmental and agricultural laws have traditionally operated in parallel, often without sufficient coordination, despite the intrinsic connection between ecological health and agricultural productivity. A holistic approach calls for convergence through ecosystem-based management, watershed planning, biodiversity conservation, and climate adaptation strategies that recognize the interdependence of land, water, forests, and farming systems. Legislative harmonization and effective inter-ministerial coordination are indispensable to prevent policy contradictions and ensure that sustainability objectives are consistently reflected across governance structures. The future trajectory of sustainability law lies in embedding ecological ethics at the core of decision-making processes. Environmental impact assessments must expand beyond narrow project-specific evaluations to incorporate cumulative ecological impacts, climate implications, and social justice considerations. Development initiatives should be evaluated not only in terms of economic growth but also in light of their long-term environmental consequences and their effects on vulnerable communities. Similarly, agricultural subsidy regimes should be redesigned to promote crop diversification, soil regeneration, water conservation, and organic practices, rather than reinforcing resource-intensive monocultures that contribute to ecological degradation.

Judicial interpretation, legislative reform, and participatory governance collectively play a transformative role in shaping this integrated framework. Courts can reinforce principles such as precaution, public trust, and accountability, while legislatures can modernize outdated statutes to align with contemporary sustainability goals.

Community participation ensures that local knowledge systems and grassroots concerns are incorporated into policymaking, fostering inclusive and democratic governance. Central to this integrated vision is the principle of intergenerational equity. Law and policy must safeguard the rights of future generations by preventing irreversible environmental harm and unsustainable resource exploitation. By harmonizing environmental protection, agricultural reform, and social justice within a coherent legal structure, sustainability can evolve from an inspirational ideal into a durable foundation for equitable and responsible development.

7.12 Conclusion

Legal frameworks governing environmental and agricultural sustainability form the normative backbone of holistic and responsible living. In India, the evolution of sustainability law reflects a dynamic interplay between constitutional principles, statutory enactments, judicial interpretation, and policy innovation. The Constitution lays the foundational ethos by recognizing environmental protection as integral to the right to life and by imposing duties upon both the State and citizens to safeguard natural resources. Building upon this constitutional vision, a wide array of environmental statutes, biodiversity regulations, agricultural reforms, and climate-related policies has progressively shaped a comprehensive—though still evolving legal architecture. Together, these instruments reflect a growing recognition that environmental integrity and agricultural resilience are inseparable pillars of national development.

Over the decades, judicial intervention has played a transformative role in strengthening sustainability jurisprudence. Courts have expanded the scope of environmental rights, enforced accountability for ecological harm, and introduced principles such as precaution, polluter pays, and sustainable development into domestic law. These doctrinal developments have infused environmental governance with normative clarity and moral authority. At the same time, legislative initiatives addressing soil conservation, water management, forest protection, biodiversity preservation, and climate mitigation have sought to align agricultural practices with ecological limits. Policy measures promoting organic farming, renewable energy in agriculture and climate-resilient crops further illustrate the State's commitment to integrating sustainability within development planning.

Yet, despite this substantial progress, the implementation gap remains a persistent challenge. Laws that appear robust on paper often encounter obstacles in practice due to fragmented administration, overlapping jurisdictions, limited institutional capacity, and insufficient coordination among regulatory bodies. Environmental clearances may be weakened by procedural formalities, monitoring mechanisms may lack transparency, and enforcement agencies may face resource constraints. In the agricultural sector, small and marginal farmers frequently encounter barriers in accessing sustainability schemes, technical support, and financial incentives. The disconnect between policy formulation and grassroots realities dilutes the transformative potential of sustainability law.

Sustainable living requires that law transcend its conventional regulatory function and operate as an ethical compass guiding social and economic behavior. Environmental degradation, biodiversity loss, and climate instability are not merely technical issues; they are moral concerns that question patterns of consumption, production, and governance. Legal frameworks must therefore encourage a culture of ecological responsibility while ensuring equity and justice. Integrating environmental protection with agricultural resilience is indispensable for ensuring food security, preserving rural livelihoods, and maintaining climate stability. Unsustainable agricultural intensification characterized by excessive chemical inputs, groundwater depletion, and monoculture practices threatens long-term productivity and ecological balance. Conversely, environmentally sound farming practices strengthen soil health, conserve water, and enhance resilience against climate shocks.

As ecological crises intensify globally, legal systems must evolve toward greater coherence, accountability, and inclusivity. Climate change, transboundary pollution, biodiversity decline, and water scarcity transcend administrative and political boundaries, demanding coordinated responses at local, national, and international levels. Harmonizing environmental and agricultural legislation through integrated planning, ecosystem-based management, and climate adaptation strategies is essential to avoid policy contradictions. Regulatory frameworks must incorporate scientific research, data-driven monitoring, and adaptive governance mechanisms capable of responding to emerging environmental risks. At the same time, transparency and public participation must be strengthened to enhance democratic legitimacy and institutional trust. Interdisciplinary integration is equally critical. Sustainability law must draw upon environmental science, agricultural economics, public health, and social justice to design comprehensive solutions. For example, the intersection between pesticide regulation and public health, or between water governance and rural livelihoods, illustrates the interconnected nature of sustainability challenges. Legal reform should therefore adopt a systems-based approach that recognizes the interdependence of ecological, economic, and social dimensions. Agricultural subsidies and development incentives must be recalibrated to reward conservation-oriented practices rather than resource-intensive production models. Fiscal policies, market instruments, and technological innovation should operate in synergy with environmental regulation to create a supportive ecosystem for sustainable transformation.

The principle of intergenerational equity remains central to the normative foundation of sustainability law. Policymaking must safeguard the rights and interests of future generations by preventing irreversible ecological damage and resource depletion. Development strategies focused solely on short-term economic gains risk imposing disproportionate environmental costs on those yet to be born. By embedding long-term ecological considerations within legislative and policy frameworks, the law can promote responsible stewardship of natural resources. This forward-looking orientation ensures that progress today does not compromise the ecological security and social well-being of tomorrow.

Equally significant is the recognition that sustainability is a shared responsibility. The State bears primary responsibility for enacting and enforcing laws, formulating policies, and ensuring institutional accountability. The judiciary plays a crucial role in interpreting constitutional mandates, protecting environmental rights, and correcting administrative lapses. Farmers, industries, and local communities are essential stakeholders whose actions directly influence environmental outcomes. Citizens, through conscious consumption patterns and civic engagement, contribute to shaping a culture of sustainability. Collaborative governance—anchored in participatory democracy enables diverse actors to contribute to environmental stewardship and agricultural resilience. Adaptive governance emerges as a defining feature of a sustainable legal order. Environmental conditions, technological innovations, and socio-economic realities are constantly evolving. Legal systems must therefore remain flexible, responsive, and open to reform. Periodic review of statutes, incorporation of emerging scientific knowledge, and continuous capacity-building within institutions are necessary to ensure relevance and effectiveness. Digital governance tools, transparent data-sharing platforms, and community-based monitoring can further enhance accountability and citizen participation.

In brief, the journey toward environmental and agricultural

sustainability is both complex and imperative. India's legal framework demonstrates significant strides in recognizing ecological rights, regulating agricultural practices, and embedding sustainability within constitutional values. However, the transformative potential of these laws depends upon effective implementation, institutional integrity, and collective commitment. Sustainability law must function not merely as a mechanism of control but as a guiding framework that harmonizes economic development with ecological preservation and social justice. By fostering coherence, accountability, inclusivity, and intergenerational responsibility, legal systems can ensure that environmental stewardship and agricultural prosperity reinforce rather than undermine one another. Through adaptive governance and participatory engagement, the law can serve as a durable foundation for a sustainable, equitable and resilient future.

Legal Framework for environmental and agricultural sustanibility

PART A: MULTIPLE CHOICE QUESTIONS (MCQS)

1. The concept of sustainable living is primarily based on which principle?

A. Unlimited economic expansion

B. Intergenerational equity and ecological balance

C. Rapid industrialization without regulation

D. Privatization of natural resources

Correct Answer: B

2. In the Indian constitutional framework, environmental protection has been judicially linked primarily with which fundamental right?

A. Right to equality under Article 14

B. Right to freedom of speech under Article 19

C. Right to life under Article 21

D. Right against exploitation under Article 23

Correct Answer: C

3. Article 48A of the Constitution of India directs the State to:

A. Promote industrial growth

B. Protect and improve the environment and safeguard forests and wildlife

C. Increase agricultural exports

D. Establish private environmental agencies

Correct Answer: B

4. The Environment (Protection) Act, 1986 was enacted largely in response to which major industrial disaster?

A. Chernobyl nuclear accident

B. Fukushima nuclear disaster

C. Bhopal Gas Tragedy

D. Minamata mercury poisoning

Correct Answer: C

5. Which legal principle requires that environmental harm be prevented even in the absence of complete scientific certainty?

A. Absolute liability principle

B. Precautionary principle

C. Strict liability principle

D. Territorial sovereignty principle

Correct Answer: B

6. The Protection of Plant Varieties and Farmers' Rights Act, 2001 primarily aims to:

A. Ban genetically modified crops

B. Promote industrial agriculture

C. Balance breeders' rights with farmers' traditional rights

D. Replace traditional seeds with hybrid seeds

Correct Answer: C

7. Which legislation in India provides an institutional framework for managing climate-related disasters affecting agriculture?

A. National Food Security Act, 2013

B. Disaster Management Act, 2005

C. Water Act, 1974

D. Forest Conservation Act, 1980

Correct Answer: B

8. The principle of Common but Differentiated Responsibilities (CBDR) recognizes that:

A. All countries must bear equal environmental responsibilities

B. Developed countries bear greater historical responsibility for environmental degradation

C. Only developing countries must protect the environment

D. Environmental responsibility belongs solely to international organizations

Correct Answer: B

9. The National Green Tribunal (NGT) was established primarily to:

A. Promote agricultural subsidies

B. Resolve environmental disputes efficiently through specialized adjudication

C. Regulate international environmental treaties

D. Conduct environmental research

Correct Answer: B

10. Which emerging technological approach helps optimize the use of water, fertilizers, and pesticides in agriculture through data-driven monitoring?

A. Monoculture farming

B. Precision agriculture

C. Slash-and-burn cultivation

D. Industrial monocropping

Correct Answer: B

PART B: THEORY QUESTIONS

1. Discuss the role of law as the architectural framework for achieving sustainable living in modern societies.

2. Explain the constitutional foundations of environmental and agricultural sustainability in India with reference to Fundamental Rights, Directive Principles, and Fundamental Duties.

3. Trace the historical evolution of environmental legislation in India and analyze its significance for sustainable development.

4. Critically examine the role of the Indian judiciary in developing the doctrine of sustainable development.

5. Discuss the legal mechanisms regulating agricultural sustainability in India, particularly with reference to seed regulation, land reforms, and chemical input control.

6. Examine the relationship between climate change and agricultural law in India, highlighting key policy and legal responses.

7. Analyze the impact of international environmental agreements on domestic environmental and agricultural governance.

8. Evaluate the role of governance institutions such as Pollution Control Boards, Biodiversity Authorities, and the National Green Tribunal in implementing sustainability laws.

9. Discuss the emerging role of technology and innovation in promoting sustainable agriculture and environmental protection, along with the legal challenges involved.

10. Identify the major challenges in the implementation of sustainability laws in India and suggest possible legal and institutional reforms to address them.

Chapter 8

Law, Technology and Social Change

Dr. Dushyant Kumar
Associate Professor, Faculty of Law, Madhav University, Sirohi

The relationship between law, technology, and social change has become one of the defining characteristics of modern governance. Technological innovations are transforming economic systems, communication networks, governance structures, and environmental management practices across the globe. These changes require corresponding legal frameworks capable of regulating emerging technologies while safeguarding human rights, social justice, and environmental sustainability. This chapter examines the dynamic interaction between law and technology in shaping social transformation, with particular emphasis on the Indian legal context. It explores theoretical perspectives on law as an instrument of social change, the impact of technological innovation on legal systems, and the regulatory challenges posed by digital technologies, artificial intelligence, and biotechnology. The discussion also highlights the role of environmental technologies in promoting sustainable development and examines the legal mechanisms necessary to ensure ethical and responsible technological governance. Through analysis of statutory provisions, judicial precedents, and policy frameworks, the chapter argues that law must evolve as an adaptive and participatory instrument capable of guiding technological progress toward inclusive and sustainable social outcomes. Ultimately, the chapter demonstrates that effective integration of law and technology is essential for addressing contemporary challenges such as digital inequality, environmental degradation, and socio-economic transformation.

8.1 Introduction: Interrelationship between Law, Technology and Social Transformation

Human civilization has evolved through a dynamic interaction between technological advancement and institutional regulation. Technology continuously reshapes the ways in which societies produce goods, communicate ideas, organize governance, and structure economic relationships. Law, on the other hand, provides the normative and regulatory framework through which these technological transformations are interpreted, managed, and directed toward collective welfare. The relationship between law and technology is therefore neither incidental nor secondary; rather, it forms one of the most fundamental dimensions of social evolution. As new technologies emerge, they transform social institutions and human behaviour, thereby necessitating corresponding legal responses that ensure stability, fairness, and accountability. In this sense, the interaction between law, technology and social change represents a continuous process in which each element influences and reshapes the others. Historically, technological revolutions have consistently triggered profound transformations in social structures and legal systems. The agricultural revolution, which marked the transition from nomadic lifestyles to settled farming communities, introduced new forms of property relations and resource management. This shift required the development of legal rules governing land ownership, inheritance, and agricultural production. As communities became increasingly organized around agriculture, legal systems evolved to regulate water usage, communal land management, and trade in agricultural commodities. These early forms of regulation demonstrate how technological changes in production systems inevitably generate the need for legal institutions capable of managing emerging economic and social relationships.

The industrial revolution represented another transformative moment in the relationship between technology and law. The introduction of mechanized production, factory systems, and mass industrialization dramatically altered labour relations and economic organization. Industrialization produced unprecedented economic growth but also created new social challenges such as urban overcrowding, labour exploitation, unsafe working conditions, and environmental pollution. In response to these challenges, governments introduced labour laws, industrial safety regulations, environmental protections, and social welfare policies. Legal institutions thus became central instruments for mitigating the negative consequences of industrial technological change while preserving its economic benefits. The development of labour law, occupational safety regulations, and industrial dispute resolution mechanisms illustrates how legal frameworks evolved to address the social impacts of industrialization.

In the contemporary era, the world is experiencing a technological transformation of comparable magnitude through the digital revolution. Advances in information technology, artificial intelligence, biotechnology, robotics, and digital communication have profoundly altered the nature of economic activities, governance systems, and social interactions. Digital technologies have revolutionized communication by enabling instantaneous global connectivity through the internet, social media platforms, and mobile networks. Similarly, data-driven technologies have transformed business models, enabling new forms of digital commerce, online financial services, and automated decision-making systems. These technological developments have created unprecedented opportunities for economic development, knowledge dissemination, and democratic participation. However, they have also generated complex legal challenges that existing regulatory frameworks often struggle to address.

The rapid pace of technological innovation has intensified the need for adaptive and forward-looking legal frameworks capable of managing the risks associated with emerging technologies. Issues such as data privacy, cyber security, digital identity, algorithmic bias, and intellectual property protection illustrate the complex regulatory challenges posed by modern technological systems. Digital platforms collect and process vast quantities of personal information, raising concerns about privacy rights and data protection. Cybercrime has emerged as a major global threat, affecting financial systems, government institutions, and individual users. Artificial intelligence systems increasingly influence decision-making processes in sectors such as finance, healthcare, law enforcement, and public administration. While these technologies offer significant benefits, they also raise questions about accountability, transparency, and ethical governance.

Law therefore plays a critical role in mediating the relationship between technological innovation and social welfare. It establishes regulatory structures that govern the development, deployment, and use of technological systems while safeguarding individual rights and public interests. Legal frameworks ensure that technological progress occurs within socially acceptable boundaries and that the benefits of innovation are distributed in an equitable manner. At the same time, law must avoid imposing excessive restrictions that could stifle creativity and hinder technological advancement. The challenge for legal systems lies in striking a delicate balance between encouraging innovations and preventing potential harms associated with unregulated technological development.

The concept of law as an instrument of social change has been widely discussed in sociological jurisprudence. Legal scholars have emphasized that law does not merely reflect existing social realities but actively shapes social behaviour and institutional development. Technological change often acts as a catalyst for social transformation, compelling legal institutions to adapt in order to maintain social order and justice. In many instances, law functions as a mechanism through which societies negotiate the ethical and social implications of new technologies.

Regulatory frameworks governing biotechnology, environmental technologies, and digital communication systems illustrate how law mediates complex interactions between innovation, ethics and public welfare. In modern governance systems, technology has also become an essential tool for implementing legal and administrative functions. Governments increasingly rely on digital platforms to deliver public services, manage regulatory processes, and facilitate citizen participation. This transformation, often described as e-governance or digital governance, has significantly improved administrative efficiency and transparency. Digital platforms enable governments to process large volumes of data, streamline bureaucratic procedures, and expand access to essential services such as healthcare, education, and social welfare programs. However, the adoption of digital governance systems also raises legal concerns related to data protection, cyber security, and digital exclusion. Ensuring that technological innovations enhance democratic accountability rather than undermine it remains a central challenge for modern legal systems.

The Indian legal landscape provides a compelling illustration of how law responds to technological change and contributes to social transformation. Over the past two decades, India has experienced rapid growth in digital infrastructure, mobile connectivity, and information technology industries. Government initiatives aimed at promoting digital inclusion and technological innovations have transformed governance structures and economic activities. Legislative frameworks such as the Information Technology Act, 2000, provide legal recognition for electronic records, digital signatures, and online transactions. This legislation represents a significant milestone in the development of cyber law in India and reflects the growing importance of digital technologies in modern economic and administrative systems.

Judicial institutions have also played an important role in shaping the legal response to technological change in India. Courts frequently confront complex questions involving privacy rights, digital surveillance, and technological governance. Judicial interpretation of constitutional principles has expanded the scope of fundamental rights in response to emerging technological realities. For example, the recognition of the right to privacy as an integral component of the right to life and personal liberty has profound implications for data protection and digital governance policies. Such judicial developments illustrate how constitutional law evolves in response to technological advancements and changing societal expectations. Another important dimension of the relationship between law and technology involves environmental sustainability. Technological innovation plays a crucial role in addressing environmental challenges such as climate change, pollution, and resource depletion. Renewable energy technologies, waste management systems, and sustainable agricultural practices offer potential solutions for reducing environmental degradation while supporting economic development. However, the successful implementation of these technologies depends on supportive legal frameworks that encourage innovation while ensuring environmental protection. Environmental laws, climate policies, and regulatory incentives are therefore essential for promoting sustainable technological development.

In addition to environmental governance, technology also influences social structures and cultural norms. Digital communication platforms have transformed patterns of social interaction, enabling individuals to connect and exchange information across geographical boundaries. Social media networks have expanded opportunities for civic participation and political engagement but have also created new challenges such as misinformation, online harassment, and digital manipulation of public opinion. Legal frameworks regulating online speech, digital platforms, and electronic media must therefore address complex questions related to freedom of expression, public order, and democratic accountability.

Technological innovation also affects labour markets and economic organization. Automation, robotics, and artificial intelligence are transforming traditional employment structures by replacing certain forms of manual and routine labour while creating new opportunities in technology-driven industries. This transformation raises important legal and policy questions concerning labour rights, social security systems, and workforce retraining programs. Legal frameworks must evolve to ensure that workers affected by technological displacement receive adequate protection and opportunities for skill development.

The relationship between law, technology, and social change is therefore characterized by continuous interaction and mutual influence. Technology introduces new possibilities for economic growth, social development, and environmental protection, while law provides the institutional framework through which these possibilities are realized and regulated. At the same time, social values and ethical considerations shape the development of both technological systems and legal institutions. Public debates surrounding privacy rights, environmental protection, and technological ethics demonstrate how societal norms influence the regulatory choices made by governments and legal authorities. In the context of sustainable living, the integration of law and technology assumes particular significance. Achieving sustainable development requires innovative technological solutions capable of addressing environmental challenges while supporting economic and social progress. At the same time, legal frameworks must ensure that these technologies are developed and implemented in a manner consistent with ecological integrity, social justice, and intergenerational equity. The concept of sustainable living emphasizes the need for holistic approaches that integrate environmental protection, economic development, and social welfare. Law and technology together play a crucial role in achieving this balance by guiding innovation toward sustainable outcomes.

Furthermore, the global nature of technological innovation necessitates international cooperation in legal governance. Issues such as cyber security, climate change, and digital commerce transcend national boundaries and require coordinated regulatory responses. International legal frameworks and multilateral agreements therefore play an increasingly important role in shaping domestic regulatory policies. Countries must align their national laws with international norms while preserving their sovereign capacity to address local social and economic priorities. In conclusion, the interrelationship between law, technology, and social transformation represents a central feature of modern governance. Technological innovations continuously reshape economic systems, social interactions, and environmental management practices, creating both opportunities and challenges for societies around the world. Law functions as a guiding framework that regulates technological development, protects individual rights, and promotes social welfare. In the rapidly evolving technological landscape of the twenty-first century, legal systems must remain flexible, adaptive, and responsive to emerging challenges. By integrating technological innovation with principles of justice, sustainability, and democratic governance, law can play a transformative role in shaping a more equitable and resilient future.

8.2 Law as an Instrument of Social Change

Law has long been regarded as one of the most effective instruments for directing social change and regulating the evolution of societal institutions. In every organized society, law functions not merely as a mechanism for maintaining order but also as a transformative tool that shapes social behavior, redistributes rights and responsibilities, and guides societal progress toward collective welfare. The dynamic relationship between law and social change has been extensively examined by scholars of jurisprudence, particularly within the framework of sociological jurisprudence. This perspective emphasizes that law cannot remain static in a rapidly evolving society; rather, it must continuously adapt to changing social, economic, and technological conditions. As societies encounter new challenges arising from modernization, globalization, and technological innovation, legal institutions must evolve in order to maintain justice, stability, and social equilibrium. Consequently, law becomes both a reflection of social change and a catalyst that actively shapes the direction and character of societal transformation.

One of the most influential theoretical contributions to understanding law as a tool of social transformation comes from Roscoe Pound's concept of **"social engineering."** Pound argued that the primary function of law is to balance competing interests within society and to harmonize individual freedoms with collective welfare. According to this theory, law should operate as an instrument through which social institutions are organized in a manner that maximizes human well-being while minimizing social conflict. By designing legal rules that accommodate diverse social interests, legislators and judges can guide societal development in a rational and equitable manner. In this sense, law does not simply regulate human conduct; it actively constructs the institutional framework through which social justice and economic progress can be achieved. Pound's theory remains highly relevant in the contemporary world, particularly in the context of technological transformations that constantly redefine the boundaries of social interaction and economic activity.

Technological change often acts as a powerful catalyst for social transformation, and it is within this context that the role of law as an instrument of social change becomes particularly significant. Emerging technologies frequently disrupt existing patterns of communication, commerce, and governance, thereby creating new social relationships that existing legal frameworks may not adequately address. For instance, the rapid expansion of digital communication platforms has fundamentally altered traditional notions of privacy, freedom of expression, and intellectual property. The internet has created unprecedented opportunities for information exchange and global connectivity, but it has also generated new legal challenges such as cybercrime, digital surveillance, online harassment, and data exploitation. Legal systems must therefore reinterpret traditional legal doctrines or develop new legislative frameworks to address these emerging challenges. Through this process, law becomes an adaptive mechanism that guides technological development while safeguarding fundamental rights and societal values.

The interaction between law and technological change is not limited to regulating emerging risks; it also involves promoting innovation and facilitating socio-economic development. Governments often use legal frameworks to encourage technological progress by providing incentives, regulatory support, and institutional infrastructure for innovation. Intellectual property laws, for example, protect the rights of inventors and creators by granting exclusive rights over their inventions and creative works. Such protections encourage investment in research and development while ensuring that technological advancements contribute to economic growth. Similarly, legal frameworks governing digital infrastructure, telecommunications, and electronic commerce create an enabling environment for technological entrepreneurship and innovation. By shaping the regulatory landscape within which technology operates, law can guide innovation toward socially beneficial outcomes. In the Indian context, law has historically played a central role in promoting social transformation and addressing structural inequalities. From the period of independence onwards, the Indian Constitution and subsequent legislative enactments have been designed to establish a just and equitable social order. Constitutional provisions relating to fundamental rights, directive principles of state policy, and social justice objectives have provided the foundation for progressive legal reforms aimed at improving the socio-economic conditions of marginalized communities. Over time, legislative measures addressing issues such as environmental protection, consumer rights, digital governance, and social welfare have demonstrated how law can respond to evolving societal challenges and technological developments.

One of the most important aspects of law as an instrument of social change in India is the proactive role played by the judiciary. Indian courts, particularly the Supreme Court, have often interpreted constitutional provisions in a progressive manner in order to address emerging social realities. Through the doctrine of judicial activism and the expansion of public interest litigation, the judiciary has played a crucial role in advancing social justice and protecting fundamental rights. Courts have recognized that constitutional principles must be interpreted dynamically in light of changing social and technological conditions. This interpretive approach allows legal institutions to respond to contemporary challenges while preserving the core values of constitutional democracy.

A significant example of judicial intervention in response to technological change is the recognition of the **right to privacy as a fundamental right** by the Supreme Court of India in the landmark case of ***Justice K.S. Puttaswamy v. Union of India (2017)***. In this historic judgment, the Court held that privacy is an intrinsic component of the right to life and personal liberty under Article 21 of the Constitution. This decision has far-reaching implications for digital governance, data protection, and technological regulation in India. As digital technologies increasingly collect and process personal data, protecting individual privacy has become a critical legal concern. By affirming privacy as a fundamental right, the judiciary established a constitutional framework that guides legislative and regulatory measures related to digital technologies and data governance.

The recognition of privacy rights also reflects the broader role of law in protecting individual autonomy in an increasingly technology-driven society. Digital platforms, social media networks, and online databases collect vast amounts of personal information, raising concerns about surveillance, data misuse, and algorithmic manipulation. Legal frameworks governing data protection and cyber security must therefore ensure that technological innovation does not undermine fundamental human rights. In recent years, India has taken significant steps toward establishing comprehensive data protection regulations aimed at safeguarding personal information while enabling responsible data-driven innovation. In addition to protecting individual rights, law also functions as an instrument for promoting social welfare through regulatory incentives and policy initiatives. Governments frequently employ legal mechanisms to encourage technological solutions that address social and environmental challenges. For instance, legal frameworks promoting renewable energy technologies have played a crucial role in advancing sustainable development objectives. By providing subsidies, tax incentives, and regulatory support for solar and wind energy projects, governments can accelerate the transition toward cleaner energy systems. Such policies demonstrate how law can guide technological innovation toward environmentally responsible outcomes.

Similarly, legal initiatives aimed at expanding digital infrastructure have contributed to social inclusion and economic development. In India, government programs designed to promote digital connectivity and electronic governance have significantly improved access to public services and information. Digital platforms enable citizens to interact with government institutions, access welfare programs, and participate in administrative processes more efficiently. By establishing legal frameworks that regulate electronic transactions, digital authentication, and online service delivery, the state can create a more transparent and accountable governance system. Another important dimension of law as an instrument of social change involves addressing the socio-economic implications of technological innovation. Automation and artificial intelligence are transforming labour markets by replacing certain forms of routine labour while creating new employment opportunities in technology-driven industries. While technological innovation can enhance productivity and economic growth, it may also lead to job displacement and widening socio-economic inequalities. Legal frameworks governing labour rights, social security systems, and workforce retraining programs must therefore evolve in order to protect workers affected by technological disruption. By designing policies that facilitate skill development and workforce adaptation, governments can ensure that technological progress contributes to inclusive economic development.

Law also plays a vital role in shaping societal attitudes and cultural norms. Legal reforms often signal shifts in societal values and encourage behavioural changes that promote social progress. For example, environmental laws designed to reduce pollution and conserve natural resources reflect a growing societal commitment to ecological sustainability. Similarly, regulations governing digital communication and online behaviour aim to create a safer and more responsible digital environment. Through education, enforcement, and public awareness campaigns, legal institutions can influence social behaviour and encourage citizens to adopt practices consistent with broader societal goals.

The global dimension of technological change further reinforces the importance of law as an instrument of social transformation. Technological innovations frequently transcend national boundaries, creating challenges that require coordinated international responses. Issues such as cyber security, digital commerce, intellectual property protection, and environmental sustainability require collaborative legal frameworks that facilitate cooperation among nations. International agreements and regulatory standards therefore play a crucial role in shaping domestic legal policies and guiding technological development at the global level.

Despite its transformative potential, law alone cannot bring about social change without effective implementation and societal participation. Legal reforms must be supported by institutional capacity, administrative efficiency, and public awareness in order to achieve meaningful impact. In many cases, progressive legislation fails to produce desired outcomes due to inadequate enforcement mechanisms or limited access to legal remedies. Strengthening institutional frameworks and promoting legal literacy among citizens are therefore essential components of effective social transformation. Moreover, the relationship between law and social change is inherently reciprocal. While law can influence societal behaviour and institutional development, social movements and public opinion often drive legal reforms. Grassroots activism, civil society organizations, and public advocacy campaigns play an important role in highlighting social injustices and demanding legal change. In the context of technological governance, public debates concerning privacy rights, digital surveillance, and artificial intelligence ethics have significantly influenced policy discussions and regulatory initiatives.

In the era of rapid technological advancement, the role of law as an instrument of social change is more important than ever before. Emerging technologies present both unprecedented opportunities and complex challenges that require thoughtful regulatory responses. Legal institutions must therefore adopt flexible and forward-looking approaches that accommodate innovation while protecting fundamental rights and social values. By integrating principles of justice, sustainability, and human dignity into technological governance, law can ensure that technological progress contributes to inclusive and equitable social development. In conclusion, law serves as a powerful mechanism through which societies navigate the complexities of technological transformation and social evolution. By balancing competing interests, protecting fundamental rights, and promoting innovation, legal systems play a central role in shaping the direction of social change. In the Indian context, constitutional principles, legislative reforms, and judicial interpretations have collectively demonstrated the capacity of law to respond to emerging technological realities while advancing broader societal objectives. As technological innovation continues to reshape economic and social structures, the continued evolution of legal frameworks will remain essential for ensuring that progress occurs in a manner consistent with democratic values, social justice, and sustainable development.

8.3 Technological Innovation and Legal Evolution

Technological innovation has consistently acted as one of the most powerful forces driving the evolution of legal systems across the world. As societies adopt new technologies that transform economic activities, communication networks, governance practices, and cultural interactions, existing legal frameworks inevitably encounter situations for which they were not originally designed. Law, being a dynamic social institution, must therefore evolve in response to technological progress. The relationship between technological advancement and legal development is thus reciprocal in nature: while technology reshapes social behaviour and institutional structures, law responds by redefining norms, establishing regulatory frameworks, and ensuring that innovation operates within socially acceptable boundaries. Throughout history, legal systems have been compelled to adapt to major technological shifts, from the printing press and industrial machinery to modern digital technologies and artificial intelligence. Each technological revolution has generated new opportunities and risks, requiring legal institutions to reinterpret existing doctrines and formulate new regulatory mechanisms.

In the contemporary era, the digital revolution represents one of the most significant catalysts for legal evolution. The widespread use of the internet, mobile communication systems, and digital platforms has dramatically altered the way individuals interact, conduct business, and access public services. Electronic commerce, online banking, digital contracts, and social media communication have become integral components of modern economic and social life. These developments have expanded opportunities for global connectivity and economic growth but have also raised complex legal questions related to jurisdiction, privacy, cyber security, intellectual property, and digital identity. Traditional legal principles developed for physical transactions and territorial jurisdictions often struggle to address the borderless nature of digital interactions. As a result, legislatures and courts have been required to reinterpret legal doctrines and enact new laws to regulate the rapidly evolving digital landscape.

India provides a notable example of legal adaptation to technological change through the enactment of the Information Technology Act, 2000. This legislation was introduced to provide legal recognition to electronic records, digital signatures, and online transactions, thereby facilitating the growth of electronic commerce and digital governance. Prior to the enactment of this law, the legal validity of electronic documents and digital agreements remained uncertain under traditional contract and evidence laws. The Information Technology Act addressed these concerns by establishing a comprehensive legal framework for electronic communication and digital authentication. In addition to recognizing electronic transactions, the Act also introduced provisions aimed at preventing cybercrime and protecting digital infrastructure. Offences such as unauthorized access to computer systems, identity theft, cyber fraud, and data manipulation were formally recognized within the legal framework. By establishing regulatory mechanisms for cyber security and digital commerce, the legislation played a critical role in enabling

India's transition toward a digitally connected economy.

Judicial interpretation has also contributed significantly to the evolution of legal frameworks in response to technological advancements. Courts frequently encounter disputes involving new technologies that existing legislation may not explicitly address. In such situations, judges interpret constitutional principles and statutory provisions in a manner that accommodates technological realities while safeguarding fundamental rights. The recognition of the right to privacy as a fundamental right by the Supreme Court of India has had profound implications for digital governance and data protection. As technological systems increasingly rely on large-scale data collection and algorithmic processing, protecting individual privacy has become an essential legal concern. Judicial recognition of privacy rights has therefore influenced the development of regulatory frameworks governing digital data, surveillance practices and information security.

Technological innovation is not limited to digital communication systems; it also extends to fields such as biotechnology, medical research, and genetic engineering. Advances in biotechnology have opened new possibilities for improving agricultural productivity, developing medical treatments, and addressing global food security challenges. However, these innovations also raise complex ethical and legal questions concerning bio safety, environmental protection, and intellectual property rights. Genetic modification of crops, for example, may enhance agricultural yields and resistance to pests, but it may also create ecological risks and socio-economic concerns related to farmers' rights and biodiversity conservation. Legal frameworks governing biotechnology must therefore strike a careful balance between promoting scientific innovation and safeguarding ecological sustainability and ethical considerations.

In India, legislation such as the Protection of Plant Varieties and Farmers' Rights Act, 2001, reflects efforts to address these challenges by recognizing both the intellectual property rights of plant breeders and the traditional knowledge of farmers. The law attempts to create a balanced system that encourages agricultural innovation while preserving biodiversity and protecting the livelihoods of farming communities. Similarly, bio safety regulations and environmental impact assessment procedures aim to evaluate the potential risks associated with genetically modified organisms before their commercial use. These legal measures illustrate how technological advancements in biotechnology necessitate comprehensive regulatory frameworks capable of addressing scientific, environmental, and socio-economic concerns simultaneously.

Technological innovation has also transformed environmental governance and climate policy. The global challenge of climate change has stimulated the development of new technologies designed to reduce greenhouse gas emissions, promote energy efficiency, and encourage sustainable resource management. Renewable energy technologies such as solar power, wind energy, and bioenergy have emerged as critical tools for transitioning toward a low-carbon economy. However, the widespread adoption of these technologies depends significantly on supportive legal and policy frameworks. Governments must establish regulatory mechanisms that encourage investment in renewable energy while ensuring environmental safeguards and equitable access to resources. In India, various legislative and policy initiatives have been introduced to promote renewable energy development and sustainable environmental practices. Regulatory incentives such as subsidies, feed-in tariffs, and renewable purchase obligations encourage industries and consumers to adopt clean energy technologies. Environmental laws governing pollution control, waste management, and conservation of natural resources also play a crucial role in guiding technological development toward sustainable outcomes. By integrating environmental objectives with technological innovation, legal systems can help address ecological challenges while promoting economic growth.

Despite these regulatory efforts, technological innovation often progresses at a pace that exceeds the ability of legislative processes to respond effectively. New technologies frequently emerge faster than governments can design comprehensive regulatory frameworks, resulting in temporary legal gaps or uncertainties. For instance, developments in artificial intelligence, block chain technology, and digital currencies have created regulatory challenges that many legal systems are still attempting to address. In such circumstances, legal institutions must adopt adaptive governance strategies that allow regulatory frameworks to evolve in response to rapidly changing technological environments.

Adaptive governance involves the use of flexible regulatory approaches that encourage innovation while maintaining oversight and accountability. Instead of relying solely on rigid legislative rules, governments may adopt regulatory sandboxes, pilot programs, and consultative policy processes that enable experimentation and stakeholder engagement. These mechanisms allow policymakers to assess the potential benefits and risks of new technologies before implementing comprehensive regulatory measures. By involving experts from diverse fields such as technology, law, economics, and environmental science, adaptive governance approaches promote more informed and balanced policy decisions.

Stakeholder participation is another essential element of effective technological regulation. The development and implementation of new technologies affect a wide range of social groups, including businesses, consumers, researchers, and local communities. Inclusive policy-making processes that involve these stakeholders can help ensure that regulatory frameworks address diverse interests and concerns. Public consultations, expert committees, and interdisciplinary research initiatives contribute to the formulation of legal policies that reflect both technological realities and societal values.

Another significant challenge in regulating technological innovation relates to the global nature of modern technological systems. Digital platforms, online commerce networks, and communication infrastructures frequently operate across national borders, making it difficult for individual countries to regulate them independently. Issues such as cross-border data flows, international cybercrime, and digital trade require cooperative regulatory frameworks at the international level. International agreements and collaborative governance mechanisms therefore play an increasingly important role in shaping national legal responses to technological change. Furthermore, technological innovation also raises broader questions concerning ethical governance and human rights protection. Technologies such as artificial intelligence, facial recognition systems, and predictive analytics have the potential to enhance administrative efficiency and public safety, but they also create risks related to surveillance, discrimination, and misuse of personal data. Legal frameworks must therefore incorporate ethical safeguards that ensure technological systems operate in a manner consistent with democratic values and human dignity. Transparency, accountability, and oversight mechanisms are essential components of responsible technological governance.

The continuous interaction between technological innovation and legal evolution highlights the need for interdisciplinary collaboration in policy-making and regulatory design. Legal scholars, technologists, policymakers, and social scientists must work together to develop regulatory frameworks that balance innovation with social responsibility. Such collaboration ensures that technological development remains aligned with broader societal objectives such as economic inclusion, environmental sustainability, and protection of fundamental rights. In conclusion, technological innovation serves as a powerful catalyst for the evolution of legal systems, compelling legislatures, courts, and regulatory institutions to adapt to rapidly changing social and economic conditions. From digital communication networks and electronic commerce to biotechnology and renewable energy technologies, each new wave of innovation introduces opportunities for societal advancement while simultaneously presenting complex regulatory challenges. Legal frameworks must therefore remain flexible, responsive, and forward-looking in order to guide technological development in a manner that promotes social welfare, environmental sustainability, and ethical governance. By integrating technological progress with robust legal oversight, societies can ensure that innovation contributes to inclusive development and sustainable living in an increasingly interconnected world.

8.4 Digital Technology and Legal Governance

The rapid advancement of digital technology has fundamentally transformed governance systems across the world, redefining the relationship between the state and its citizens. Governments increasingly rely on digital platforms, electronic databases, and information networks to deliver public services, regulate economic activities, and communicate with citizens. This transformation, widely known as digital governance or e-governance, represents a shift from traditional bureaucratic administration toward technology-enabled governance structures that prioritize efficiency, transparency, and accessibility. Digital governance involves the integration of information and communication technologies into governmental processes in order to streamline administrative procedures, enhance service delivery, and strengthen democratic accountability. As societies become increasingly interconnected through digital networks, legal frameworks must evolve to regulate technological systems and ensure that digital governance operates within the principles of constitutional democracy, human rights, and public accountability.

Digital governance has significantly altered the way public institutions perform administrative functions. Traditionally, governance systems relied heavily on paper-based records, physical documentation, and in-person interactions between government officials and citizens. These processes were often time-consuming, inefficient, and vulnerable to bureaucratic delays or corruption. The adoption of digital technologies has enabled governments to automate many administrative tasks, create centralized data repositories, and offer online platforms for public services. Citizens can now access government schemes, apply for official documents, and interact with public authorities through digital portals without the need for physical visits to government offices. This transformation has not only increased administrative efficiency but also improved transparency by reducing opportunities for discretionary decision-making and bureaucratic manipulation.

In India, the expansion of digital governance has been strongly supported by national initiatives aimed at strengthening technological infrastructure and promoting digital inclusion. One of the most prominent initiatives is the **Digital India Programme**, which seeks to transform the country into a digitally empowered society and knowledge-based economy. The program focuses on expanding internet connectivity, promoting digital literacy, and enabling electronic delivery of government services. Through digital platforms, citizens can access services such as identity verification, financial transactions, tax payments, social welfare schemes, and public grievance mechanisms. These initiatives demonstrate the potential of digital technology to improve governance by making public services more accessible, efficient, and transparent.

However, the increasing reliance on digital technologies in governance also raises complex legal challenges that must be addressed through comprehensive regulatory frameworks. One of the most significant concerns associated with digital governance is the protection of personal data and privacy. Digital platforms collect vast amounts of personal information from citizens, including financial records, biometric identifiers, and communication data. While such information can enhance the efficiency of governance systems, it also creates risks related to surveillance, data breaches, and misuse of personal information. Legal frameworks governing digital governance must therefore establish clear rules regarding data collection, storage, processing, and sharing. Ensuring that personal information is handled in a secure and responsible manner is essential for maintaining public trust in digital governance systems.

A landmark development in the Indian constitutional framework concerning digital governance and privacy rights is the decision of the Supreme Court in ***Justice K.S. Puttaswamy v. Union of India (2017)***. In this historic judgment, the Court unanimously recognized the right to privacy as a fundamental right protected under Article 21 of the Constitution, which guarantees the right to life and personal liberty. The Court emphasized that privacy is an essential component of human dignity and autonomy, particularly in the context of modern digital technologies that enable extensive data collection and surveillance. By affirming privacy as a fundamental constitutional value, the judgment established a legal foundation for regulating data protection and digital governance in India. The decision has influenced legislative efforts aimed at creating comprehensive data protection laws that balance technological innovation with individual rights and freedoms.

Cyber security represents another critical dimension of digital governance and legal regulation. As governments increasingly rely on digital infrastructure to manage administrative processes and public services, the security of these systems becomes a matter of national importance. Cyber attacks targeting government databases, financial institutions, and public infrastructure can disrupt essential services and compromise sensitive information. Cyber threats such as hacking, phishing, identity theft, and ransom ware attacks pose significant risks to both governmental institutions and individual citizens. Effective cyber security frameworks require legal provisions that criminalize cyber offences, establish investigative mechanisms, and promote cooperation between law enforcement agencies and technological experts. The development of robust cyber security laws and institutions is therefore essential for protecting digital governance systems from malicious activities.

The legal regulation of cybercrime is particularly important in an era where digital technologies facilitate cross-border communication and financial transactions. Cybercriminals often operate across international jurisdictions, making it difficult for national authorities to investigate and prosecute offences effectively. Legal frameworks must therefore incorporate mechanisms for international cooperation, mutual legal assistance, and cross-border data sharing. In India, the Information Technology Act and related regulatory provisions provide a legal foundation for addressing cyber offences and establishing institutional mechanisms for cyber security management. However, as cyber threats continue to evolve in complexity and scale, legal frameworks must also adapt through continuous reforms and technological collaboration.

Digital technology has also significantly influenced the functioning of judicial institutions and the administration of justice. Courts around the world are increasingly adopting technological solutions to improve the efficiency and accessibility of legal processes. The concept of **digital justice** or **technology-enabled justice** involves the use of electronic systems for case management, online filing of legal documents, and virtual hearings conducted through video conferencing platforms. These innovations have transformed traditional courtroom procedures by reducing delays, minimizing administrative burdens, and expanding access to justice for individuals who may face geographical or economic barriers in approaching courts.

In India, the judiciary has gradually embraced digital technology through initiatives such as the **e-Courts Mission Mode Project**, which aims to modernize court infrastructure and improve judicial efficiency through digital systems. Electronic filing systems enable lawyers and litigants to submit legal documents online, while digital case management platforms allow courts to track and manage cases more effectively. Virtual hearings conducted through video conferencing technology have become increasingly common, particularly during periods when physical court proceedings may be disrupted by external circumstances such as public health emergencies. These technological developments demonstrate how digital governance can enhance the accessibility and responsiveness of judicial institutions. Another significant aspect of digital governance relates to transparency and accountability in public administration. Digital platforms enable governments to publish information related to policies, budgets, and administrative decisions in real time, thereby strengthening mechanisms for public oversight. Citizens can use online portals to monitor government projects, submit feedback, and report grievances, creating new opportunities for participatory governance. Legal frameworks supporting the right to information and open data policies further reinforce the principles of transparency and democratic accountability within digital governance systems.

However, the benefits of digital governance must be balanced against the risks of digital exclusion and technological inequality. Access to digital platforms often depends on the availability of reliable internet connectivity, digital literacy, and technological infrastructure. In many regions, particularly in rural and economically disadvantaged communities, limited access to digital resources may prevent citizens from fully benefiting from technology-enabled governance systems. Legal and policy frameworks must therefore ensure that digital governance initiatives promote inclusivity rather than reinforcing existing socio-economic disparities. Investments in digital infrastructure, education, and community-based training programs are essential for bridging the digital divide and ensuring equitable access to digital services. Furthermore, ethical considerations play an increasingly important role in the legal governance of digital technologies. Automated decision-making systems, algorithmic governance, and artificial intelligence applications are increasingly used in administrative processes such as welfare distribution, law enforcement, and public resource management. While these technologies can improve efficiency and accuracy, they also raise concerns regarding transparency, accountability, and potential biases in algorithmic decision-making. Legal frameworks must therefore establish safeguards that ensure automated systems operate fairly, transparently, and in accordance with fundamental rights.

The evolution of digital governance also underscores the importance of interdisciplinary collaboration between legal experts, technologists, policymakers, and civil society organizations. Designing effective regulatory frameworks for digital technologies requires a deep understanding of both legal principles and technological processes. Collaborative policy-making processes involving diverse stakeholders can help ensure that regulatory measures address practical challenges while upholding democratic values and ethical standards. In conclusion, digital technology has emerged as a transformative force in modern governance, reshaping administrative processes, public service delivery, and judicial systems. The integration of digital platforms into governance structures has the potential to enhance transparency, efficiency, and citizen participation, thereby strengthening democratic institutions. However, the increasing reliance on digital technologies also introduces complex legal challenges related to privacy protection, cybersecurity, data governance, and digital inclusion. Legal frameworks must therefore evolve continuously in order to regulate technological systems effectively while safeguarding constitutional rights and societal values. By integrating technological innovation with robust legal oversight and ethical governance principles, digital technologies can serve as powerful tools for advancing good governance, social justice, and sustainable development in the digital age.

8.5 Artificial Intelligence and Legal Challenges

Artificial Intelligence (AI) has emerged as one of the most transformative technological innovations of the twenty-first century, fundamentally altering the way societies function and institutions operate. AI refers to the development of computer systems capable of performing tasks that typically require human intelligence, such as decision-making, pattern recognition, language processing, and predictive analysis. Rapid advancements in machine learning, deep learning, and data analytics have enabled AI systems to process vast amounts of information and perform complex functions with remarkable efficiency. As a result, AI technologies are increasingly being deployed across a wide range of sectors, including healthcare, finance, transportation, agriculture, law enforcement, and public administration. These technologies have the potential to enhance productivity, improve decision-making processes, and address complex societal challenges. However, alongside these benefits, AI also introduces significant legal, ethical, and regulatory challenges that demand careful consideration by lawmakers, policymakers, and judicial institutions.

One of the most prominent legal challenges associated with AI involves questions of accountability and liability. Traditional legal systems are designed around the assumption that human actors are responsible for their actions and can be held accountable for any harm they cause. However, AI systems often operate autonomously or semi-autonomously, making decisions based on algorithms and data inputs rather than direct human instructions. When such systems malfunction or produce harmful outcomes, determining who should be held legally responsible becomes a complex issue. For instance, if an autonomous vehicle causes an accident, it may be difficult to determine whether liability should rest with the manufacturer, the software developer, the operator, or the owner of the vehicle. Similarly, in sectors such as healthcare or financial services, AI-driven decision-making systems may influence critical outcomes affecting human lives and economic stability. Legal frameworks must therefore evolve to clarify the responsibilities of different stakeholders involved in the design, development, and deployment of AI technologies.

Another major concern arising from the widespread adoption of AI relates to algorithmic bias and discrimination. AI systems rely heavily on data for training and decision-making processes. If the data used to train these systems contains biases or reflects existing social inequalities, the resulting algorithms may perpetuate or even amplify discriminatory outcomes. For example, AI-based recruitment systems may inadvertently favor certain demographic groups if the training data reflects historical hiring patterns that are biased against marginalized communities. Similarly, facial recognition technologies have been criticized for exhibiting higher error rates when identifying individuals from certain ethnic or racial backgrounds. Such biases can undermine principles of equality and fairness, particularly when AI systems are used in areas such as law enforcement, employment screening, credit assessment, or public service delivery. Legal frameworks must therefore incorporate safeguards that ensure transparency, fairness, and accountability in algorithmic decision-making processes. Regulatory measures may require organizations to conduct regular audits of AI systems, disclose algorithmic methodologies, and implement mechanisms for correcting biased outcomes.

Transparency and explain ability represent additional challenges in the governance of artificial intelligence. Many advanced AI systems operate through complex machine learning models that are difficult to interpret even for their developers. These systems are often referred to as "black box" algorithms because their internal decision-making processes are not easily understandable or explainable. The lack of transparency in AI decision-making raises significant legal and ethical concerns, particularly when such systems are used to make decisions affecting fundamental rights and opportunities. For example, individuals denied credit, employment, or public benefits based on algorithmic assessments may have limited ability to challenge these decisions if the underlying logic of the algorithm remains opaque. Legal frameworks governing AI must therefore emphasize the importance of explainable and accountable systems that allow individuals to understand how decisions affecting them are made. Ensuring transparency in algorithmic processes is essential for maintaining public trust in AI technologies and for upholding principles of procedural fairness.

Artificial intelligence also presents complex questions concerning intellectual property rights. Traditional intellectual property laws, particularly copyright law, are designed to protect creative works produced by human authors. However, AI systems are increasingly capable of generating original content, including music, literature, artwork, and even scientific research outputs. This development raises fundamental questions about the ownership and legal protection of AI-generated works. If an AI system creates a piece of music or a written article, it is unclear whether copyright protection should be granted and, if so, who should hold those rights. Possible claimants may include the developer of the AI system, the organization that deployed it, or the individual who provided input data. Existing copyright frameworks may struggle to accommodate such scenarios because they were developed in an era when creative works were exclusively associated with human authorship. Consequently, legal scholars and policymakers are increasingly exploring new regulatory models that address the unique challenges posed by AI-generated content.

In addition to intellectual property concerns, AI technologies also raise important questions related to privacy and data protection. AI systems rely heavily on large datasets, often containing personal information, in order to function effectively. The collection, processing, and analysis of such data create potential risks related to unauthorized access, surveillance, and misuse of personal information. As governments and private organizations deploy AI technologies for purposes such as predictive policing, healthcare diagnostics, and targeted advertising, the need for robust data protection frameworks becomes increasingly urgent. Legal regulations must ensure that the use of personal data in AI systems respects fundamental rights to privacy and autonomy. This requires clear guidelines regarding data consent, storage limitations, security safeguards, and mechanisms for individuals to access and correct their personal information. Another area of legal concern involves the impact of artificial intelligence on employment and labour markets. Automation technologies powered by AI have the potential to replace certain forms of routine or repetitive work, thereby altering traditional employment patterns. While technological innovation can create new industries and job opportunities, it may also lead to displacement of workers in sectors such as manufacturing, transportation, and administrative services. The resulting economic and social consequences require thoughtful policy responses aimed at protecting workers and facilitating workforce adaptation. Labour laws, social security systems, and education policies must evolve to address the challenges posed by AI-driven automation. Governments may need to invest in re skilling and up skilling programs that enable workers to transition into new roles created by technological innovation.

The governance of artificial intelligence also involves significant ethical considerations related to human autonomy, dignity, and social responsibility. AI systems increasingly influence decisions in areas such as healthcare treatment, criminal justice, financial credit, and public resource allocation. When automated systems make decisions that significantly affect human lives, questions arise regarding the appropriate balance between human judgment and machine intelligence. Ethical governance of AI requires that human oversight remain an integral part of decision-making processes, particularly in sensitive domains involving fundamental rights. Legal frameworks must ensure that AI technologies are used in a manner that respects human dignity and promotes social welfare rather than undermining democratic values. Recognizing these challenges, governments and international organizations have begun developing regulatory frameworks and ethical guidelines for the responsible development and use of artificial intelligence. International bodies such as the United Nations, the Organization for Economic Co-operation and Development (OECD), and UNESCO have proposed principles emphasizing transparency, accountability, human rights protection, and sustainability in AI governance. These principles encourage governments to adopt regulatory approaches that promote innovation while ensuring ethical safeguards. Similarly, several countries have introduced national strategies and policy frameworks aimed at fostering responsible AI development.

In the Indian context, discussions surrounding AI governance are gaining increasing importance as the country continues to expand its digital infrastructure and technological capabilities. Government initiatives promoting artificial intelligence in sectors such as healthcare, agriculture, and education demonstrate the potential of AI to address developmental challenges. At the same time, policymakers are exploring legal mechanisms to ensure that the deployment of AI technologies remains consistent with constitutional values and human rights principles. Issues such as data protection, algorithmic accountability, and ethical AI governance are likely to shape future legislative reforms in India's technological regulatory landscape.

Despite the growing recognition of the need for AI regulation, achieving an appropriate balance between innovation and regulation remains a complex task. Overly restrictive regulations may hinder technological progress and limit the potential benefits of AI, while insufficient regulation may expose individuals and societies to significant risks. Policymakers must therefore adopt flexible and adaptive regulatory approaches that encourage responsible experimentation while maintaining adequate safeguards. Regulatory sandboxes, collaborative policy frameworks, and interdisciplinary research initiatives can help governments better understand emerging AI technologies and design effective legal responses. In conclusion, artificial intelligence represents a powerful technological development with the potential to reshape nearly every aspect of modern society. Its applications offer significant benefits in areas such as healthcare, economic development, environmental management, and public administration. However, the deployment of AI also raises complex legal challenges related to accountability, algorithmic bias, transparency, intellectual property, privacy protection, and labour market disruption. Addressing these challenges requires the development of comprehensive legal frameworks that integrate technological innovation with ethical governance and human rights protection. As AI continues to evolve and expand its influence across various sectors, legal systems must remain proactive and adaptive in order to ensure that technological progress contributes to social justice, democratic accountability, and sustainable development.

8.6 Technology, Environment and Sustainable Development

Technological innovation has emerged as a crucial driver in addressing contemporary environmental challenges and advancing the broader objectives of sustainable development. As global populations grow and economic activities intensify, pressure on natural resources and ecological systems continues to increase. Issues such as climate change, biodiversity loss, water scarcity, pollution, and unsustainable agricultural practices pose serious threats to the stability of ecosystems and human well-being. In this context, technological advancements offer promising solutions that can reduce environmental degradation while simultaneously supporting economic productivity and social development. Technologies such as renewable energy systems, waste recycling mechanisms, sustainable agricultural practices, and environmental monitoring tools provide innovative ways to balance developmental aspirations with ecological protection. However, the successful implementation of these technologies depends significantly on robust legal frameworks that regulate their development, ensure environmental accountability, and promote responsible use of natural resources.

One of the most prominent areas where technology contributes to sustainable development is the transition toward renewable energy sources. Fossil fuel–based energy systems have long been associated with greenhouse gas emissions, air pollution, and environmental degradation. Renewable energy technologies such as solar power, wind energy, hydroelectric generation, and bioenergy present cleaner alternatives capable of reducing carbon emissions and mitigating climate change. Advances in photovoltaic technology, energy storage systems, and smart grid infrastructure have significantly improved the efficiency and accessibility of renewable energy solutions. These technological developments enable countries to diversify their energy sources while reducing dependence on fossil fuels. However, the adoption and expansion of renewable energy systems require supportive legal and policy frameworks that encourage investment, establish regulatory standards, and ensure environmental safeguards.

Legal frameworks play a fundamental role in facilitating the transition toward sustainable energy systems. Governments implement policies such as renewable energy subsidies, feed-in tariffs, tax incentives, and renewable purchase obligations to encourage the adoption of clean energy technologies. Environmental regulations also establish standards for emissions control and energy efficiency, thereby creating incentives for industries to adopt environmentally friendly technologies. In many jurisdictions, climate change legislation and national energy policies incorporate targets for renewable energy generation and carbon emission reductions. Such regulatory measures provide the institutional framework necessary for integrating technological innovation into broader environmental governance strategies.

In the Indian context, technological innovation has been increasingly integrated into environmental governance and climate policy. India has adopted several policy initiatives aimed at promoting renewable energy development and addressing environmental challenges associated with rapid industrialization and urbanization. Programs encouraging solar energy deployment, wind power generation, and energy-efficient technologies demonstrate the country's commitment to transitioning toward sustainable energy systems. Government initiatives focusing on solar power generation in rural areas, for example, not only reduce dependence on fossil fuels but also improve energy access for communities that previously lacked reliable electricity supply. By combining technological innovation with policy incentives, such initiatives illustrate how environmental sustainability and socio-economic development can be pursued simultaneously. In addition to renewable energy technologies, innovations in waste management and recycling systems also play an essential role in promoting sustainable development. Rapid urbanization and industrial growth have led to increasing volumes of solid waste, electronic waste, and industrial by-products. Improper waste disposal can contaminate soil, water, and air, thereby posing serious threats to environmental and public health. Technological solutions such as advanced recycling systems, waste-to-energy plants, and biodegradable materials offer effective methods for reducing waste accumulation and recovering valuable resources from discarded materials. For instance, waste-to-energy technologies convert municipal waste into electricity or heat, thereby reducing landfill usage while generating renewable energy. Similarly, innovations in biodegradable packaging materials can significantly reduce plastic pollution in natural ecosystems.

However, technological solutions in waste management must be accompanied by effective legal regulations to ensure safe and environmentally responsible practices. Environmental laws governing waste management establish standards for waste segregation, recycling, transportation, and disposal. These regulations are essential for preventing environmental contamination and promoting the circular economy model, in which resources are reused and recycled rather than discarded. The concept of extended producer responsibility, which holds manufacturers accountable for the environmental impacts of their products throughout their lifecycle, represents an important legal mechanism for encouraging sustainable production and consumption patterns.

Technological innovation also plays a significant role in advancing sustainable agricultural practices. Agriculture remains one of the most resource-intensive sectors of the global economy, requiring large quantities of water, land, and chemical inputs. Conventional farming practices often contribute to soil degradation, water pollution, and loss of biodiversity. Emerging technologies such as precision agriculture, satellite-based crop monitoring, and climate-resilient crop varieties offer new opportunities to enhance agricultural productivity while minimizing environmental impacts. Precision agriculture, for instance, uses data analytics and sensor technologies to optimize the use of fertilizers, pesticides, and irrigation systems, thereby reducing resource waste and environmental contamination.

Legal frameworks governing agricultural sustainability are essential for guiding the adoption of such technologies. Environmental regulations addressing soil conservation, water resource management, and chemical input control ensure that technological innovations in agriculture are implemented responsibly. Policies promoting organic farming, sustainable irrigation techniques, and biodiversity conservation further contribute to the development of environmentally friendly agricultural systems. By integrating technological advancements with regulatory oversight, governments can encourage farming practices that protect natural ecosystems while maintaining food security. Another important aspect of technology in environmental governance involves the use of digital monitoring systems and environmental data analysis. Satellite imaging, remote sensing technologies, and geographic information systems (GIS) enable governments and environmental organizations to monitor ecological changes in real time. These technologies can track deforestation, monitor air and water quality, detect illegal mining activities, and assess the impacts of climate change on natural ecosystems. Such monitoring systems enhance the capacity of regulatory agencies to enforce environmental laws and respond to ecological threats more effectively. Digital environmental monitoring also facilitates evidence-based policymaking by providing accurate and comprehensive data on environmental conditions.

Despite the numerous benefits associated with technological solutions for environmental sustainability, it is important to recognize that technology alone cannot guarantee ecological balance. Without appropriate legal oversight and regulatory controls, technological development may inadvertently create new environmental risks. For example, the extraction of minerals required for manufacturing renewable energy technologies such as solar panels and batteries may lead to environmental degradation if mining activities are not properly regulated. Similarly, large-scale renewable energy projects such as hydropower dams or wind farms may disrupt local ecosystems and affect wildlife habitats. These challenges highlight the importance of comprehensive environmental impact assessment procedures that evaluate the ecological consequences of technological projects before their implementation.

Environmental impact assessments serve as a crucial legal mechanism for ensuring that technological developments are environmentally sustainable. These assessments require project developers to analyze potential ecological effects, consider alternative approaches, and implement mitigation measures to minimize environmental harm. By incorporating environmental considerations into planning and decision-making processes, such regulatory frameworks help balance technological innovation with ecological preservation. Public participation in environmental decision-making further strengthens the legitimacy and effectiveness of sustainability initiatives by allowing communities to express concerns and contribute to policy discussions.

Sustainable development also requires international cooperation in the regulation of technology and environmental governance. Climate change, biodiversity conservation, and pollution control are global challenges that transcend national boundaries. International agreements and environmental treaties encourage countries to adopt environmentally responsible technologies and share knowledge related to sustainable development practices. Collaborative research initiatives, technology transfer mechanisms, and financial support for green technologies enable developing countries to participate in global sustainability efforts. Legal frameworks at both national and international levels must therefore work together to promote technological solutions that address shared environmental challenges.

In conclusion, technological innovation plays a pivotal role in advancing environmental protection and sustainable development by offering solutions that reduce ecological degradation and enhance resource efficiency. Renewable energy systems, waste management technologies, sustainable agricultural practices, and environmental monitoring tools demonstrate the transformative potential of technology in addressing environmental challenges. However, the success of these technological solutions depends heavily on the presence of strong legal frameworks that regulate their development and ensure environmental accountability. Environmental laws, climate policies, and sustainability regulations provide the institutional foundation necessary for integrating technological innovation with ecological governance. At the same time, policymakers must remain vigilant to ensure that technological advancements do not create unintended environmental consequences. Achieving sustainable development therefore requires a holistic approach that combines technological progress with robust legal oversight, responsible governance, and active public participation. Through such integrated efforts, societies can harness the power of technology to build environmentally resilient and sustainable futures for present and future generations.

8.7 Social Implications of Technological Change

Technological change has significantly transformed modern societies, influencing social structures, cultural practices, communication patterns, and economic relationships. The rapid expansion of digital technologies, automation systems, and artificial intelligence has reshaped the ways in which individuals interact with one another and participate in social, political, and economic activities. These developments have created new opportunities for innovation and social progress, but they have also generated complex social challenges that require careful legal and policy responses. As technology becomes increasingly integrated into everyday life, its impact on social relations, employment structures, information dissemination, and access to opportunities continues to grow. Consequently, legal frameworks must adapt to ensure that technological advancement contributes to social welfare while protecting individuals from emerging risks associated with digital transformation.

One of the most visible social impacts of technological change is the transformation of communication and information sharing. Digital communication technologies such as the internet, Smartphone's and social media platforms have revolutionized the way individuals connect with one another. These platforms enable instant communication across geographical boundaries and provide individuals with unprecedented access to information. Social media networks, online forums, and digital news platforms have expanded opportunities for public participation in political discourse and civic engagement. Citizens can now express opinions, mobilize support for social causes, and participate in public debates through digital channels that were previously unavailable. This democratization of information has strengthened freedom of expression and broadened public awareness of social and political issues.

However, the expansion of digital communication has also introduced significant challenges related to misinformation, hate speech, and online harassment. Social media platforms can be used to disseminate false information, manipulate public opinion, and promote divisive narratives that undermine social harmony. The rapid spread of misinformation during political events, public health crises, or social conflicts demonstrates how digital technologies can influence collective perceptions and decision-making processes. In addition, online harassment, cyber bullying, and hate speech have become growing concerns, particularly for vulnerable groups such as women, minorities, and young people. These developments highlight the need for legal frameworks that regulate harmful online behavior while preserving fundamental rights such as freedom of expression and access to information. Governments and regulatory institutions must therefore establish mechanisms to address digital misinformation, promote responsible online conduct and protect individuals from cyber harassment.

Technological change has also had a profound impact on labour markets and employment structures. Automation technologies and artificial intelligence are increasingly capable of performing tasks that were traditionally carried out by human workers. Industries such as manufacturing, logistics, customer service, and administrative support have experienced significant automation in recent years. While technological innovation can increase productivity, reduce operational costs, and create new forms of employment in emerging sectors, it can also lead to job displacement for workers engaged in routine or repetitive tasks. This transformation of labour markets raises important social and legal concerns regarding job security, income inequality, and workforce adaptation.

In response to these challenges, labour laws and social welfare policies must evolve to address the implications of technological displacement. Governments may need to introduce policies that support reskilling and upskilling initiatives, enabling workers to adapt to changing technological environments. Educational institutions and training programs play a crucial role in preparing individuals for employment opportunities in technology-driven sectors such as digital services, data analysis, renewable energy, and advanced manufacturing. At the same time, social security systems must be strengthened to provide support for workers who face temporary unemployment or economic instability due to technological transitions. By integrating labour policy reforms with technological development strategies, societies can mitigate the negative social consequences of automation while maximizing its economic benefits.

Education systems have also been deeply influenced by technological advancements. The development of online learning platforms, digital libraries, and interactive educational tools has significantly expanded access to knowledge and educational resources. Students can now participate in virtual classrooms, access global academic content, and collaborate with peers across different regions through digital platforms. These innovations have proven particularly valuable in situations where traditional educational systems face disruptions, such as during global health emergencies or natural disasters. Digital education technologies have the potential to democratize learning by providing flexible and accessible educational opportunities for diverse populations.

Despite these benefits, technological transformation in education has also exposed significant disparities related to digital infrastructure and technological literacy. Access to reliable internet connectivity, digital devices, and technological training remains uneven across different regions and socio-economic groups. Students in rural or economically disadvantaged communities may face barriers that limit their ability to benefit from digital education platforms. These disparities highlight the importance of legal and policy interventions aimed at promoting digital inclusion and equitable access to educational resources. Governments must invest in digital infrastructure development, support affordable internet access, and implement programs that enhance digital literacy among students and educators.

The broader social implications of technological change also extend to issues of equality, social justice, and inclusive development. Technological innovation can contribute to economic growth and improved living standards, but its benefits may not be distributed evenly across society. Without appropriate regulatory safeguards, technological progress can deepen existing inequalities by concentrating economic opportunities in certain sectors or regions while marginalizing others. Legal frameworks must therefore ensure that technological development aligns with principles of social equity and human rights protection. Policies promoting inclusive innovation, digital accessibility, and equitable resource distribution are essential for ensuring that technological progress benefits all segments of society. In conclusion, technological change has far-reaching social implications that influence communication, employment, education, and social equality. While digital technologies and automation systems create new opportunities for economic growth and social participation, they also present challenges related to misinformation, cyber harassment, job displacement, and digital inequality. Addressing these issues requires comprehensive legal frameworks that balance technological innovation with social responsibility and human rights protection. By adopting inclusive policies, strengthening regulatory institutions, and investing in digital infrastructure and education, societies can ensure that technological progress contributes to sustainable and equitable social development.

8.8 Future Directions: Law, Technology and Sustainable Social Transformation

As technological innovation continues to advance at an unprecedented pace, the relationship between law and technology will become increasingly significant in shaping the future of societies. Emerging technologies such as artificial intelligence, biotechnology, digital governance systems, and renewable energy innovations are rapidly transforming economic activities, social interactions, and governance structures. In this evolving environment, legal systems must develop adaptive and forward-looking regulatory frameworks capable of responding to complex technological developments and their broader societal implications. Traditional legal mechanisms often evolve slowly, while technological progress occurs rapidly, creating regulatory gaps that may expose societies to ethical, environmental, and economic risks. Therefore, future legal reforms must emphasize flexibility, responsiveness, and the capacity to address new challenges as they arise.

A key aspect of future legal development lies in strengthening interdisciplinary collaboration. Effective governance of emerging technologies requires cooperation among legal scholars, scientists, engineers, economists, policymakers, and social researchers. Such collaboration ensures that regulatory frameworks are not only legally sound but also technically informed and ethically responsible. By integrating diverse forms of expertise, policymakers can better anticipate the potential consequences of technological innovation and design regulations that promote both innovation and public welfare.

In the context of sustainable social transformation, law must play a proactive role in guiding technological development toward environmentally responsible and socially inclusive outcomes. Legal frameworks should promote the adoption of technologies that support environmental protection, resource efficiency, and climate resilience. Renewable energy systems, smart urban infrastructure, sustainable agricultural practices, and environmentally friendly industrial technologies represent important components of future sustainable development strategies. Through incentives, regulatory standards, and environmental governance mechanisms, law can encourage technological solutions that balance economic growth with ecological sustainability.

International cooperation will also be essential in addressing global technological challenges. Issues such as cyber security threats, cross-border data flows, climate change mitigation, and digital governance cannot be effectively managed by individual nations alone. Coordinated legal responses at regional and international levels will help establish shared standards and promote responsible technological development across borders. Ultimately, the future relationship between law and technology will depend on the ability of legal systems to guide innovation in a manner that protects fundamental rights, ensures social justice, and promotes sustainable development. By establishing ethical standards, encouraging responsible innovation, and strengthening global cooperation, law can play a decisive role in shaping a technologically advanced yet socially balanced future.

Conclusion

The dynamic relationship between law, technology, and social change has become one of the defining features of contemporary governance. Rapid technological advancements have transformed the ways in which societies function, influencing economic systems, social interactions, governance mechanisms, and environmental management practices. From digital communication platforms and artificial intelligence systems to renewable energy technologies and data-driven governance models, technological innovation continues to reshape the institutional and social landscape. These transformations present both opportunities and challenges for legal systems. While technology can enhance efficiency, productivity, and accessibility in various sectors, it can also create complex legal questions related to privacy, accountability, equality, and environmental sustainability. Consequently, modern legal frameworks must evolve continuously to address the emerging implications of technological progress while safeguarding fundamental rights and promoting the collective welfare of society.

In the Indian context, the interaction between law and technology is increasingly reflected in legislative reforms, judicial interpretations, and policy initiatives designed to regulate the rapidly expanding digital and technological environment. Laws governing digital transactions, data protection, cyber security, environmental sustainability, and technological governance illustrate how legal institutions are adapting to the changing realities of a technology-driven society. Judicial decisions have also played a crucial role in interpreting constitutional principles in light of technological developments, ensuring that technological advancement remains consistent with democratic values, human dignity, and the rule of law. Such developments demonstrate the capacity of legal systems to respond to societal transformation while maintaining institutional stability and constitutional integrity.

Looking ahead, effective governance in the twenty-first century will require a holistic and integrated approach that harmonizes legal regulation with technological innovation and social policy objectives. Policymakers must ensure that technological progress is guided by ethical principles, environmental responsibility, and inclusive development strategies. By establishing adaptive legal frameworks, encouraging responsible technological innovation, and protecting the rights and interests of citizens, law can play a central role in shaping a balanced and sustainable future. Ultimately, the successful integration of law and technology will determine the ability of societies to achieve social justice, economic resilience, and long-term sustainability in an increasingly complex and interconnected world.

MCQs on Law, Technology and Social Change

1. Who propounded the theory of "Social Engineering" in law?

A. Jeremy Bentham

B. John Austin

C. Roscoe Pound

D. H.L.A. Hart

2. Which Indian legislation provides legal recognition to electronic records and digital signatures?

A. Companies Act, 2013

B. Information Technology Act, 2000

C. Consumer Protection Act, 2019

D. Digital Governance Act

3. The Right to Privacy was recognized as a fundamental right by the Supreme Court of India in which case?

A. Maneka Gandhi v. Union of India

B. Justice K.S. Puttaswamy v. Union of India

C. Kesavananda Bharati v. State of Kerala

D. Shreya Singhal v. Union of India

4. Which concept refers to the use of digital technologies by governments to deliver services and interact with citizens?

A. Cyber legislation

B. E-governance

C. Administrative justice

D. Digital surveillance

5. Artificial Intelligence raises legal concerns mainly related to:

A. Agriculture and irrigation

B. Accountability and liability

C. Population growth

D. Religious freedom

6. Which of the following technologies is most closely associated with sustainable energy?

A. Nuclear weapons

B. Fossil fuel engines

C. Solar and wind power

D. Coal mining

7. Algorithmic bias in AI systems occurs when:

A. Algorithms are too slow

B. Algorithms contain errors in programming language

C. AI systems produce unfair or discriminatory outcomes

D. Computers malfunction

8. Which technological innovation has significantly transformed communication and information sharing in modern society?

A. Printing press

B. Telegraph

C. Social media platforms

D. Typewriters

9. Which of the following is a legal mechanism used to evaluate environmental impact before a project is implemented?

A. Judicial review

B. Environmental Impact Assessment (EIA)

C. Arbitration

D. Habeas Corpus

10. Sustainable development primarily aims to:

A. Increase industrial output only

B. Balance economic growth with environmental protection

C. Promote technological monopolies

D. Replace natural resources entirely

Theory Questions on Law, Technology and Social Change

1. Explain the concept of law as an instrument of social change with reference to sociological jurisprudence.

2. Discuss the relationship between technological innovation and legal evolution.

3. Examine the role of digital governance in improving transparency and administrative efficiency.

4. Analyze the legal challenges associated with Artificial Intelligence and algorithmic decision-making.

5. Discuss the importance of legal frameworks in regulating digital technologies and protecting data privacy.

6. Explain the role of technology in promoting environmental sustainability and renewable energy development.

7. Critically examine the social implications of technological change in the areas of employment, communication, and education.

8. Discuss the challenges posed by cybercrime and the role of legal systems in addressing digital security threats.

9. Evaluate the role of international cooperation in regulating emerging technologies and addressing global challenges such as cyber security and climate change.

10. Explain how law can guide technological innovation toward sustainable and socially responsible development.

Chapter 9

Sustainable Farming Practices and Technological Interventions

Sitaram Seervi1
Assistant Professor, College of Agriculture, Madhav University, Pindwara, Sirohi (Raj.)

Preeti Mahawar
Associate Professor, College of Agriculture, Madhav University, Pindwara, Sirohi (Raj.)
Author Gmail: sitaramseervi88@gmail.com

1. Introduction

Agriculture plays a central role in ensuring global food security and rural livelihoods. In countries such as India, agriculture supports a significant portion of the population and contributes substantially to GDP and employment. However, the intensification of agriculture since the Green Revolution has led to soil degradation, water scarcity, biodiversity loss and environmental pollution. Excessive use of chemical fertilizers and pesticides, mono cropping systems, and over-extraction of groundwater has raised serious sustainability concerns.

Sustainable farming has emerged as a holistic approach that integrates environmental stewardship, economic profitability, and social responsibility. Technological innovations such as precision agriculture, artificial intelligence, biotechnology, remote sensing, and renewable energy systems have strengthened sustainable agricultural practices worldwide. This chapter presents an in-depth discussion of sustainable farming principles, practices, technological interventions, policy support, challenges, and future prospects, supported by scientific references.

2. Concept and Principles of Sustainable Agriculture

Sustainable agriculture refers to farming systems that meet present needs without compromising the ability of future generations to meet their own needs (Brundt land Commission, 1987).

2.1 Core Principles

1. Conservation of natural resources
2. Economic viability
3. Social equity
4. Reduced environmental pollution
5. Enhanced resilience to climate change

According to Food and Agriculture Organization, sustainable agriculture must increase productivity while conserving ecosystems and strengthening farmers' adaptive capacity (FAO, 2013).

3. Soil Health Management

Soil health is fundamental for sustainable farming systems.

3.1 Organic Matter Management

Incorporation of farmyard manure, compost, green manure, and crop residues enhances soil organic carbon and microbial activity (Lal, 2015).

3.2 Conservation Tillage

Minimum tillage and zero tillage reduce soil erosion, improve soil aggregation, and enhance carbon sequestration (Hobbs et al., 2008).

3.3 Integrated Nutrient Management (INM)

INM combines chemical fertilizers with organic inputs and bio fertilizers to maintain soil fertility and reduce environmental risks (Gruhn et al., 2000).

4. Water Resource Management

Water-use efficiency is critical under changing climatic conditions.

4.1 Micro -Irrigation Systems

Drip and sprinkler irrigation systems significantly improve water productivity compared to traditional flood irrigation (Postel et al., 2001).

4.2 Rainwater Harvesting and Watershed Management

Watershed-based approaches enhance groundwater recharge and reduce soil erosion (Wani et al., 2009).

Government initiatives such as PMKSY in India promote efficient irrigation practices.

5. Crop Diversification and Agroecological Practices

5.1 Crop Rotation

Rotating cereals with legumes improves nitrogen availability and breaks pest cycles (Tilman et al., 2002).

5.2 Agroforestry

Agroforestry systems enhance biodiversity, improve soil fertility, and contribute to carbon sequestration (Nair, 2011).

5.3 Integrated Pest Management (IPM)

IPM reduces pesticide use by combining biological control, resistant varieties, and cultural practices. The Indian Council of Agricultural Research actively promotes IPM technologies in India.

According to Pimentel (2005), IPM can significantly reduce environmental contamination while maintaining crop productivity.

6. Organic and Natural Farming

Organic farming avoids synthetic fertilizers and pesticides and emphasizes ecological balance. Standards are regulated globally by IFOAM – Organics International.

Studies show that organic systems enhance soil biodiversity and reduce chemical residues (Reganold & Wachter, 2016). However, yield gaps may exist under certain conditions.

7. Integrated Farming Systems (IFS)

Integrated farming combines crops, livestock, poultry, fisheries, and other enterprises to optimize resource recycling and diversify income (Jayanthi et al., 2003). IFS enhances nutrient recycling, reduces production risk, and improves overall farm sustainability.

8. Technological Interventions in Sustainable Agriculture

8.1 Precision Agriculture

Precision farming utilizes GPS, sensors, GIS, and data analytics to optimize input use. Variable rate technology reduces fertilizer and pesticide overuse (Zhang et al., 2002).

8.2 Artificial Intelligence and Machine Learning

AI-driven models predict pest outbreaks, yield potential, and irrigation requirements (Kamilaris & Prenafeta - Boldú, 2018).

8.3 Internet of Things (IoT)

IoT-based sensors monitor soil moisture, temperature, and nutrient levels, improving decision-making and resource efficiency.

8.4 Remote Sensing and GIS

Satellite imagery assists in crop health monitoring, drought assessment, and land-use planning.

8.5 Biotechnology

Biotechnology develops stress-resistant and pest-resistant crop varieties. Bt cotton adoption in India significantly reduced pesticide use and increased yields (Qaim & Zilberman, 2003).

8.6 Renewable Energy in Agriculture

Solar-powered irrigation systems and biogas plants reduce dependence on fossil fuels and lower greenhouse gas emissions. Digital agricultural transformation initiatives under Digital India have enhanced rural connectivity and advisory services.

9. Climate-Smart Agriculture (CSA)

Climate change poses major risks to agricultural productivity. CSA aims to:

1. Increase productivity
2. Enhance resilience
3. Reduce greenhouse gas emissions

According to Food and Agriculture Organization (2013), CSA integrates sustainable land management, improved varieties, and risk management strategies.

10. Policy Support and Institutional Role

Government policies significantly influence sustainable agriculture adoption. In India, programs such as:

- National Mission on Sustainable Agriculture (NMSA)
- Paramparagat Krishi Vikas Yojana (PKVY)
- Pradhan Mantri Krishi Sinchai Yojana (PMKSY)

Research and extension institutions, particularly ICAR and agricultural universities, facilitate technology dissemination.

11. Challenges in Adoption

- High initial investment costs
- Limited awareness and technical knowledge
- Fragmented landholdings
- Market uncertainties
- Inadequate policy implementation

Bridging research-extension gaps is essential.

12. Conclusion

Sustainable farming represents a comprehensive approach to achieving food security, environmental conservation, and economic viability. Integration of traditional practices with technological innovations such as precision agriculture, biotechnology, AI, and renewable energy strengthens resilience and productivity. Effective policies, farmer awareness, and institutional support are crucial for widespread adoption.

Chapter 10

Agriculture Systems in a Changing Climate

An agricultural system is a combination of components which are united by some form of interaction and interdependence and which operate within a prescribed boundary to achieve a specified agricultural objective on behalf of the beneficiaries of the system.

Climate change poses a substantial threat to agricultural sustainability globally. Agriculture is a vital component of the gross domestic production of developing countries. The multifaceted impacts of climate change on agriculture, highlighting how extreme weather events such as water stress, heat waves, erratic rainfall, storms, floods, and emerging pest infestations are disrupting agricultural productivity. The socioeconomic status of farmers is particularly vulnerable to climatic extremes with future projections indicating significant increment in ambient air temperatures and unpredictable, intense rainfall patterns. Agriculture has historically relied on the extensive use of synthetic fertilizers, herbicides, and insecticides, combined with advancements in irrigation and biotechnological approaches to boost productivity. It encompasses a range of practices designed to enhance the resilience of agricultural systems, improve productivity, and reduce greenhouse gas emissions. By adopting climate-smart practices, farmers can better adapt to changing climatic conditions, thereby ensuring more sustainable and secure food production. Furthermore, it identifies key areas for future research, focusing on the development of innovative adaptation and mitigation strategies. These strategies are essential for minimizing the detrimental impacts of climate change on agriculture and for promoting the long-term sustainability of food systems.

As a culprit, agriculture drives deforestation through expansion of cropland and pasture, displacing natural forests that store carbon and support biodiversity. In many tropical regions, smallholder and commercial agriculture alike spur forest clearing for maize, soy, oil palm, and livestock, eroding ecosystem integrity and amplifying emissions. Forest conversion releases large amounts of carbon from biomass and soils, fragmenting habitats and disrupting hydrological cycles (Curtis et al., 2018; Pen drill et al., 2019). In regions where slash-and-burn is prevalent, short-term fertility gains mask long-term losses in soil organic matter and resilience. The combination of market demand, weak land-use governance, and poverty-induced subsistence expansion sustains this pattern, linking farm-level decisions to global biodiversity loss. Agriculture is also a major source of greenhouse gases, notably methane from ruminant enteric fermentation and flooded rice, nitrous oxide from synthetic and organic nitrogen inputs, and carbon dioxide from land-use change and energy use. Globally, food systems account for roughly one-third of anthropogenic GHG emissions when including supply chains (Crippa et al., 2021), with on-farm activities contributing a substantial share. Inefficient fertilizer uses leads to emissions via nitrification and denitrification, while manure mismanagement and open burning of residues add methane and carbon dioxide. Even in low-input systems, poor nutrient management can create hotspots of emissions relative to yields, underscoring the need for improved agronomy. A third pathway of culpability is soil and water degradation driven by unsustainable practices. Conventional tillage, overgrazing, and nutrient mining degrade soil structure, reduce organic carbon, and increase erosion. Over-abstraction of water for irrigation diminishes river flows and depletes aquifers, while agrochemical runoff and sedimentation impair water quality and aquatic ecosystems (FAO, 2015). In rainfed areas, bare soils and contour-insensitive plowing exacerbate runoff and flood risks. These degradative processes lower productivity over time, creating feedback loops where farmers expand further into marginal lands, perpetuating environmental harm.

As a victim, agriculture is increasingly vulnerable to climate change, which alters rainfall patterns, intensifies droughts and floods, and raises temperatures beyond crop and livestock thresholds. Yield variability has grown with shifting onset of rains and more frequent dry spells in southern Africa, while heat stress reduces grain filling and livestock performance (IPCC, 2023).

Extreme events damage infrastructure, seeds, and stored grain, and increase post-harvest losses. Smallholders with limited irrigation and financial buffers are disproportionately affected, undermining food security and incomes. Land degradation also harms agriculture by diminishing the natural capital on which it depends. Soil erosion removes fertile topsoil, salinization reduces crop suitability in poorly managed irrigated areas, and loss of soil biota weakens nutrient cycling. Desertification processes in dry lands reduce vegetation cover, expose soils to wind erosion, and lower infiltration, making drought impacts more severe (UNCCD, 2017). As soils degrade, input use efficiency declines, raising costs and risks for farmers and trapping them in low-productivity cycles. Agriculture is further victimized by rising pest and disease pressures. Warmer temperatures and altered humidity expand the ranges and life cycles of pathogens and insect pests, while extreme weather events can trigger outbreaks. The fall armyworm invasion across Africa demonstrated how climate and trade accelerate pest spread, causing significant maize losses (Day et al., 2017). Plant diseases such as cassava brown streak and banana wilt, and livestock diseases influenced by vector ecology, impose heavy burdens on farmers. Resistance to pesticides and antimicrobials compounds the challenge, requiring integrated management.

As a solution, agriculture can deliver ecosystem services that regenerate landscapes. Agroforestry systems integrate trees with crops and livestock, enhancing biodiversity, stabilizing soils, regulating microclimates, and providing pollinator habitat and fuelwood. Riparian buffers and wetlands restored within agricultural mosaics improve water quality and flood regulation, while diversified rotations foster natural pest control and resilience (Montagnini & Nair, 2004). These services not only support production but also safeguard downstream communities and ecosystems. Sustainable farming practices transform agriculture from extractive to restorative.

Conservation agriculture, minimal soil disturbance, permanent soil cover, and crop diversification builds soil organic matter, reduces erosion, and improves water infiltration, benefiting yield stability under climate stress (Kassam et al., 2009). Precision nutrient management, integrated soil fertility strategies combining organic amendments with optimized mineral inputs, and integrated pest management reduce environmental footprints while maintaining productivity. Livestock systems that adopt improved grazing management, fodder shrubs, and manure recycling enhance nutrient cycling and landscape health. Finally, agriculture can be a significant avenue for carbon sequestration. Soils and biomass in croplands and pastures can store additional carbon through practices like cover cropping, reduced tillage, residue retention, organic amendments, and rewetting of drained peatlands. Agro forestry and assisted natural regeneration increase above- and below-ground carbon stocks, while improved rice management reduces methane. Although sequestration potentials vary by climate, soil type, and management, scaling these practices across suitable contexts contributes to climate mitigation and co-benefits for fertility and water retention (Paustian et al., 2016; Smith et al., 2014).

In sum, agriculture's triple role demands integrated policy and practice shifts. Recognizing its culpability motivates curbing deforestation, emissions, and degradation; acknowledging its victimhood compels investments in adaptation and resilience; and leveraging its solutions advances ecosystem services, sustainability, and carbon storage. For countries with large smallholder sectors, aligning incentives, tenure security, extension services, and access to finance is central to unlocking a transformation that feeds people while healing the environment.

The identified applications of digital technologies in agriculture include Remote Sensing for crop monitoring, Big Data for predictive modelling of water shortages and pest outbreaks, Artificial Intelligence for pest identification and tracking, the Internet of Things for precision fertiliser management, nanotechnology for soil improvement, robots for targeted spraying, and block chain for improved soil management and supply chain transparency, among others. These technologies facilitate the precise management of resources, improve decision-making processes and enable more efficient agricultural practices. Digital technologies also help mitigate climate change by optimising inputs such as water and fertiliser, thereby reducing greenhouse gas emissions and promoting carbon sequestration.

However, there are significant barriers to the adoption of these technologies, including the digital divide, high up-front costs and complexity, as well as privacy and security concerns and the environmental impact of technology use. Future action must address these barriers by investing in infrastructure and training, ensuring financial incentives, developing scalable digital solutions tailored to local agricultural conditions, increasing digital literacy among farmers, developing comprehensive governance frameworks, and exploring the integration of multiple digital technologies. The paper contributes to advancing scientific understanding and guiding practice and policy towards sustainable agriculture in the face of climate change. It provides a call to action for a more sustainable future in the context of climate change and highlights the urgency of multi-stakeholder collaboration to create an enabling environment for the widespread adoption of these innovations, ensuring that they are accessible, cost-effective and suitable for different farming environments.

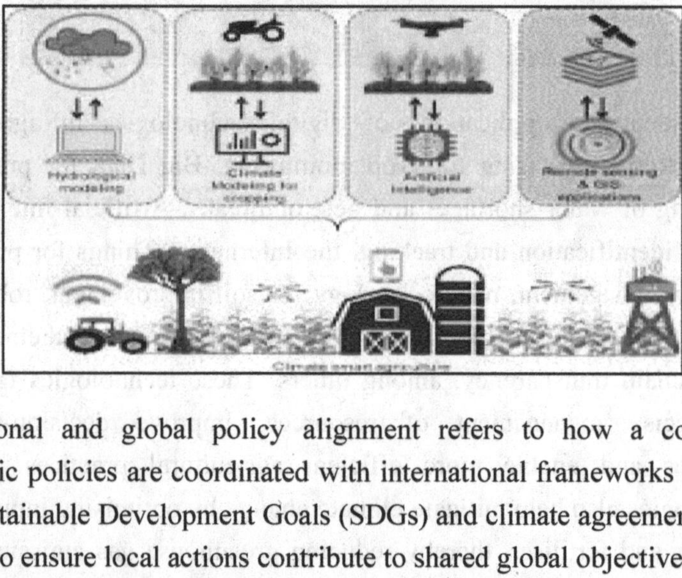

National and global policy alignment refers to how a country's domestic policies are coordinated with international frameworks such as the Sustainable Development Goals (SDGs) and climate agreements. The aim is to ensure local actions contribute to shared global objectives.

1. Alignment with the SDGs

The SDGs are a set of 17 global goals adopted by the United Nations to guide development up to 2030.

1. **Policy mapping:** Governments link national development plans to specific SDGs (e.g. health policy - SDG 3).
2. **Indicators & reporting:** Countries use SDG indicators to track progress and submit *Voluntary National Reviews*.
3. **Budget alignment:** Public spending is tagged to SDGs to ensure

resources match priorities.

4. **Stakeholder integration:** Involving local governments, private sector, and civil society.

2. Alignment with Climate Agreements

The most important climate framework today is the Paris Agreement under the UNFCCC.

1. **Nationally Determined Contributions (NDCs):** Each country sets emission reduction targets.
2. **Domestic legislation:** Climate laws, carbon pricing, renewable energy mandates.
3. **Sector integration:** Energy, transport, agriculture, and industry policies reflect climate goals.
4. **Monitoring & verification:** Emissions inventories aligned with international standards.

3. Common Challenges

- **Policy incoherence:** Economic growth policies contradict climate goals.
- **Capacity gaps:** Weak data systems for reporting.
- Short-term politics vs long-term goals.
- **Global inequality:** Developing countries need finance and technology to align effectively.

4. Why This Is Critical

Policy alignment is essential for:

- Avoiding duplicated or conflicting efforts.
- Turning global commitments into real national action.
- Ensuring that global problems (climate change, poverty, inequality) are addressed consistently across borders.

In short: Global goals set the direction; national policies deliver the results.

Chapter 11

Engineering Innovation for Social Development

Mr. Amit kumar Agarwal
Assistant professor dept of engineering madhav university sirohi

Introduction

Engineering innovation in social development entails utilizing creative thinking, smart engineering design, and resource efficiency in solving large-scale social problems like poverty, inequality, insufficient healthcare, education, clean water, energy, and livelihoods. This contrasts with conventional engineering that emphasizes performance and profit in terms of resource utilization.

Concepts like frugal engineering (doing more with less), jugaad innovation (resourceful innovation originating in India), and inclusive innovation have become more significant in solving problems in developing regions.

This is because they empower marginalized groups in society, reduce multidimensional poverty, and drive forward the United Nations Sustainable Development Goals (SDGs). These SDGs include SDG 1 No Poverty, SDG 3 Good Health, SDG 4 Quality Education, SDG 6 Clean Water, and SDG 7 Affordable Energy.

By 2026, frugal and inclusive engineering have become more prominent due to digital technology, 3D printing technology, AI technology, and public-private sector collaborations in solving problems in region like India and Africa.

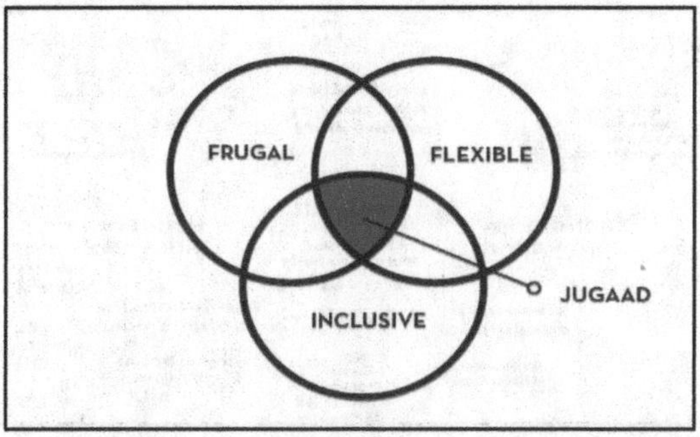

Figure: Venn diagram illustrating the core principles of Jugaad /Frugal Innovation — Frugal, Flexible, and Inclusive — overlapping to form resourceful, adaptive solutions.

Principles of Engineering for Social Impact

Key principles to guide the approach:

- View resource limitations as opportunities to innovate and use locally available resources, existing expertise, and minimized capital requirements.

-**Make it affordable:** reduce costs by 50-90% compared to traditional approaches without compromising on functionality.

- **Design for growth and flexibility:** the solution should be applicable in various low-infrastructure contexts and easily replicable in the local environment.

- **Put people first:** co-create with the community to ensure the solution remains relevant to them.

- **Commit to sustainability:** reduce negative environmental impacts and maximize positive social impacts.

These principles draw from frameworks like design thinking combined with bricolage (creative recombination of available resources).

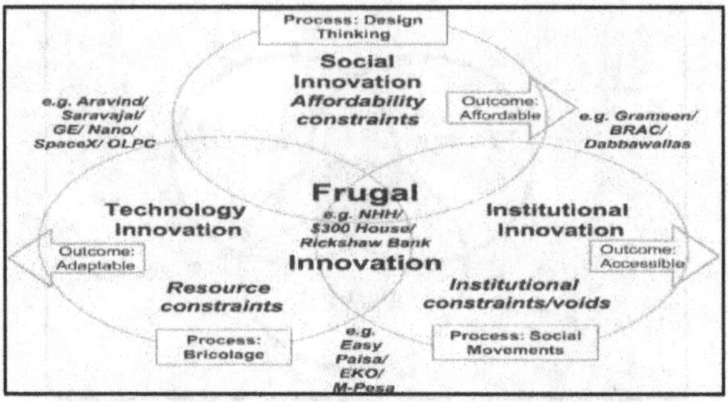

Figure: Theoretical framework of frugal innovation, showing intersections of social, technological, and institutional innovations leading to affordable, adaptable, and accessible outcomes.

3. Healthcare Access: Affordable Prosthetics and Diagnostics

Engineering has revolutionized healthcare in underserved regions of the world by providing practical tools at an affordable price. One of the notable breakthroughs is prosthetic sockets that can be customized to fit individual amputees. Traditionally, prosthetics come with an expensive price tag that is compounded by an unsatisfactory fit. With frugal engineering, medical images such as X-rays/CT scans can be used to generate digital models of amputees, develop customized prosthetic sockets, perform structural analysis, and 3D print prosthetic limbs at a fraction of the cost of traditional prosthetic limbs.

This has helped amputees in rural India and Africa walk again without incurring huge costs. Other notable innovations in healthcare include ECG machines like the GE MAC 400, which was originally developed for bus ticket printers, and artificial intelligence-based tools for TB screening.

Impact: Narrowing healthcare disparities, improving the quality of life, and helping millions of people contribute to the economy.

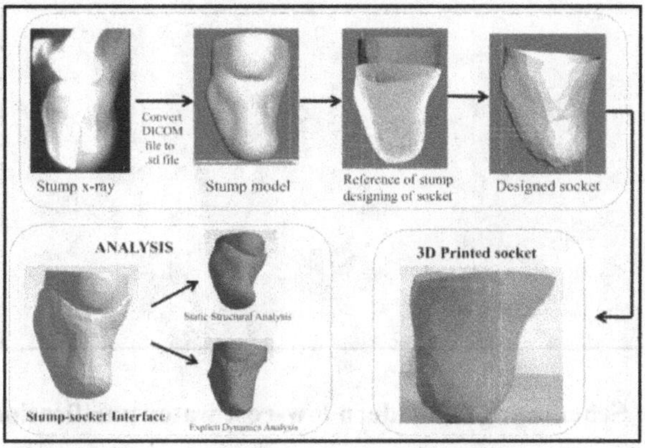

Figure: Workflow for designing and 3D-printing a patient-specific lower limb prosthetic socket, from imaging to final product with structural analysis.

4. Water and Sanitation: Frugal Purification Systems

Since potable water is still out of reach for billions of people, the focus is on frugal purification systems, especially those using local materials and requiring minimal energy. The answer could be the humble slow sand filter, with its layers of sand and the all-important schmutzdecke, the active layer of microorganisms doing all the work. Or the more modern, solar-powered versions, such as the gel filter and the clay-based refrigerators, such as the Mitti Cool, for keeping food cool without the need for electricity. Sedimentation, decantation, and a bit of coagulation result in very clean water, and in Rajasthan and parts of sub-Saharan Africa, these approaches reduce waterborne diseases by 70-90% and can be had for under $50 per household unit.

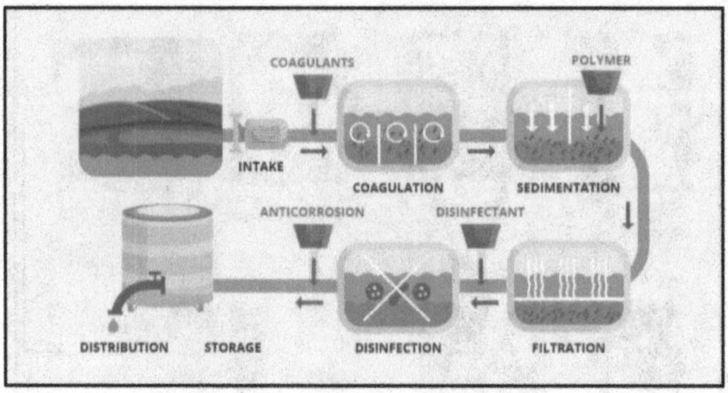

Figure: Schematic of a modern low-cost water purification process emphasizing sedimentation, coagulation, and filtration stages suitable for rural deployment.

5. Agriculture and Livelihoods: Solar-Powered Irrigation

Smallholder farmers in dry lands face the challenge of water scarcity and low energy availability. Solar-powered irrigation combines photovoltaic panels, DC power, soil moisture sensors, and automation to provide water to crops in exact amounts, without the need for the grid or fossil fuels. The outcome is more crops, with yields increasing by 30-50%, reduced labor, and the potential to grow crops throughout the year. For places like India or Africa, the system is made more accessible through pay-as-you-go or micro-financing. It also reduces greenhouse gases and is more resilient to climate changes.

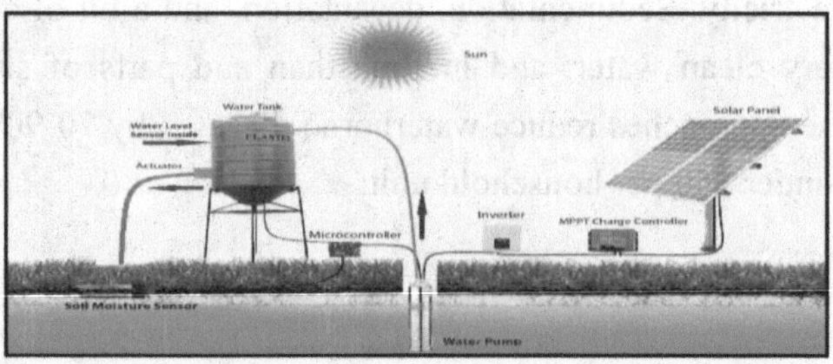

Figure: Components and layout of a solar-powered irrigation system with sensors, pumps, and controllers for efficient, off-grid farming.

6. Education and Digital Inclusion

Engineers are fueling inclusive learning through affordable tablets, offline AI learning tools, and solar-powered kiosks. Platforms are also providing content for low-literacy users and areas that are hard to reach. In Africa and India, affordable technology is helping to fill gaps and improve learning outcomes for disadvantaged children.

7. Challenges, Strategies, and Future Directions

The challenges facing engineering social development include funding, skills gaps, maintenance, and acceptance. However, the way forward includes partnerships between NGOs and governments, open-source technology, skills training, and impact measurement. In 2030, the fusion of AI, biotechnology, and frugal engineering is a glimpse into a future where breakthroughs such as bio-hybrid agriculture and health devices are possible. Engineers should be at the forefront in ensuring that social innovations are empowering and not exclusionary.

Conclusion

Social engineering is a way to transform constraints into opportunities. Engineers have been able to show that engineering can be a force for social upliftment. Engineers have been able to show their capability to innovate through approaches such as jugaad technology to create prosthetic limbs and solar-powered irrigation. Engineers have a duty to innovate not just efficiently but also inclusively to build a world where technology is used to empower humanity's most vulnerable members

Chapter 12

Smart Technology and Infrastructure System

Mr. Amit kumar Agarwal
Assistant professor dept of engineering madhav university sirohi

1. Introduction to Smart Infrastructure

Smart infrastructure refers to the integration of physical infrastructure, including roads, bridges, buildings, utilities, and energy, with advanced digital technologies to create self-monitoring, self-optimizing, and resilient urban ecosystems. Smart infrastructure refers to smart automation technologies facilitated by advanced hardware and software technologies to provide intelligent real-time decisions. Smart infrastructure essentially integrates Internet of Things sensors, Building Information Modeling, real-time data analytics, artificial intelligence, and 5G wireless communication technologies to continuously monitor physical infrastructure and optimize their performance.

Unlike traditional infrastructure, smart infrastructure provides predictive and adaptive technologies to minimize waste, reduce greenhouse gas emissions, maximize asset life, and improve safety and quality of life. The global move towards smart infrastructure development is driven by rapid urbanization, climate change, and the imperative to meet the net-zero target. By 2030, smart cities investments are expected to exceed $2 trillion annually, with Internet of Things-enabled infrastructure serving as the backbone.

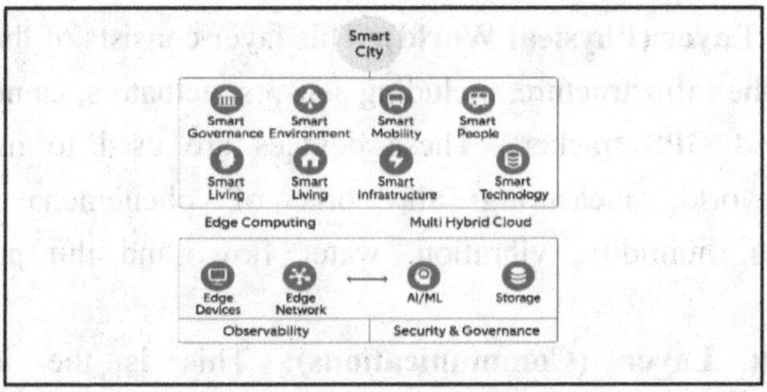

Figure 1.1: Nine key domains of a Smart City ecosystem

The Core Architecture: A Multi-Layered Framework

To grasp the way smart infrastructure works, it's useful to consider a conceptual architecture for smart infrastructure as a multi-layered stack, with each layer built upon the one below. This architecture spans the physical world of data acquisition to the digital world of data analysis and action. The International Telecommunication Union's architecture is a good one to use as a foundation, and it can be modified to show the flow of information.

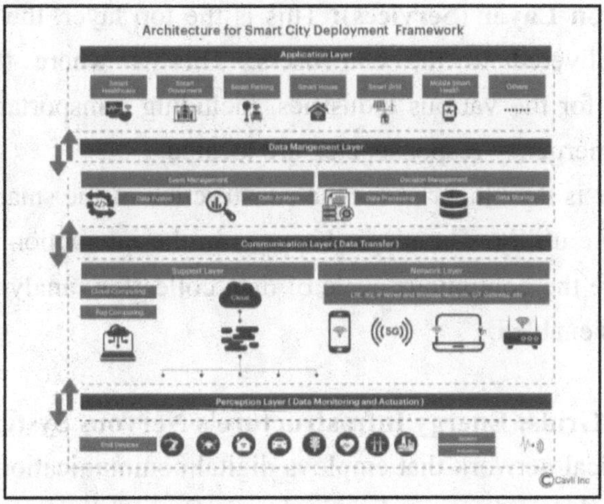

Figure:A Multi-Layer Architecture for Smart Infrastructure Systems

Sensing Layer (Physical World): This layer consists of the "terminal nodes" of the infrastructure, including sensors, actuators, cameras, RFID readers, and GPS trackers. These devices are used to monitor the physical world, measuring all sorts of phenomena, including temperature, humidity, vibration, water flow, and the presence of vehicles.

Network Layer (Communications): This is the information superhighway. This is where the wired and wireless communication networks, including 5G, Wi-Fi, and LPWAN, securely transport data to the central system from the sensing layer. Technologies such as 5G are critical to their speed and their capability to support millions of simultaneous connections.

Data & Support Layer (Intelligence): This is the layer where data is aggregated, stored, and analyzed. This is the layer where data centers are located, where AI, machine learning, and digital twins are employed to create intelligence. This is where the system becomes "smart," where patterns are recognized, where failures are predicted, where the system is optimized.

Application Layer (Services): This is the top layer, the layer where value is delivered to the end users. This is where the software applications for the various industries, including transportation, energy, buildings, emergency response, etc., are located.

The above is the blueprint for the construction of the smart system for the city or the utility. The magic happens in the interaction between the layers, where the continuous cycle of data collection, analysis, decision, and action is enabled.

2. Smart Grids: Energy Infrastructure's Nervous System

An electrical network that employs digital communication technology to continuously monitor, regulate, and optimize generation, transmission, distribution, and consumption is known as a smart grid. Demand-response programs, electric vehicles (EVs), and renewable energy sources can all be integrated thanks to its two-way power and information flow support.

Essential Elements:

1. Two-way communication in smart meters
2. Phasor measurement units (PMUs) and intelligent substations
3. Transmission lines with sophisticated sensors
4. Automation for self-healing (automatic fault isolation and rerouting)
5. Energy resources that are dispers

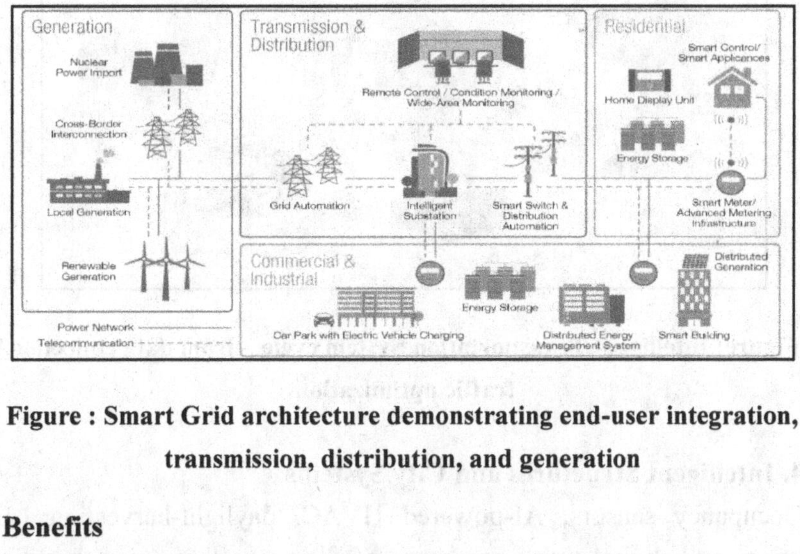

Figure : Smart Grid architecture demonstrating end-user integration, transmission, distribution, and generation

Benefits

1. Dynamic pricing can reduce peak demand by up to 30%.
2. 20–40% quicker recovery from outages
3. smooth incorporation of at least 50% renewable energy
4. decreased technical losses (from 8–12% to 4–6%).

3. Systems for Intelligent Transportation (ITS)

Roads become interconnected corridors thanks to smart mobility. Vehicle-to-infrastructure (V2I), vehicle-to-everything (V2X), cameras, radar, and artificial intelligence (AI) are all used by intelligent transportation systems to dynamically manage traffic.

Important uses:

1. Real-time traffic signal adaptation
2. Occupancy sensors and guidance apps in smart parking
3. Vibration sensors for predictive bridge and road maintenance
4. Connected corridors and autonomous shuttles

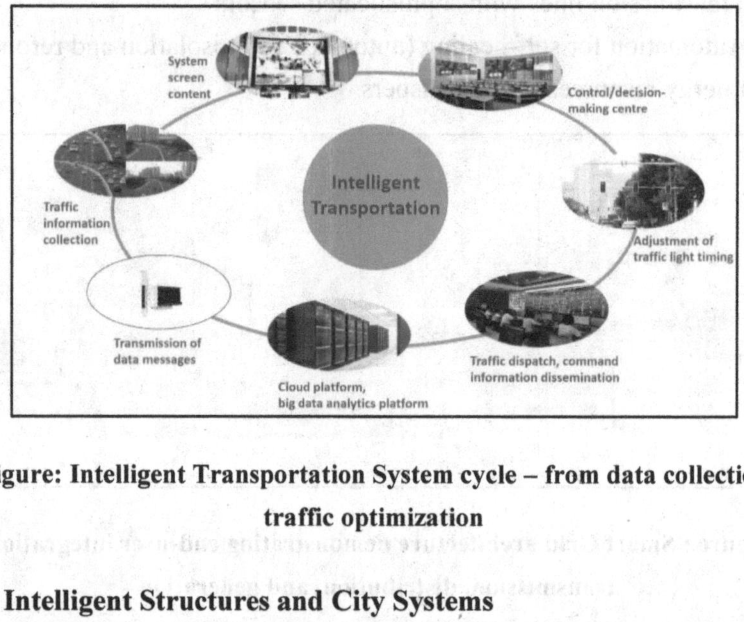

Figure: Intelligent Transportation System cycle – from data collection to traffic optimization

4. Intelligent Structures and City Systems

Occupancy sensors, AI-powered HVAC, daylight-harvesting LED lighting, and digital twins are some of the ways that smart buildings reduce energy consumption by 30 to 50%. At the city level, integrated platforms oversee:

Waste: 30% fewer truck trips thanks to fill-level sensors and dynamic routing

Water: Identifying leaks and controlling pressure (20–40% savings)

Street lighting: 50–70% energy savings with motion + ambient light control

5. Advantages, Difficulties, and Implementation Schedule

Principal Advantages:

Efficiency & Cost Savings → Lifecycle costs are cut by 20–30% thanks to predictive maintenance.

Sustainability → reduced carbon emissions by 15–40%

Self-healing grids and real-time disaster response are examples of resilience.

Better Quality of Life → Shorter commutes, safer public areas, and cleaner air

Principal Difficulties:

1. High initial investment costs

2. Vulnerabilities in cyber security (multiple entry points)

3. oncerns about data privacy

4. Absence of standards for interoperability

5. The deployment of the digital divide

Roadmap for Implementation:

Pilot programs in high-impact locations (district energy, traffic corridors)

Create cyber security frameworks and open data platforms.

Invest in public-private partnerships and workforce training.

Before a full rollout, scale using digital twins for simulation.

6. International Case Studies from a 2025 Viewpoint

With sensors installed all over the country, Singapore's Smart Nation initiative cut planning expenses by 10% thanks to digital twins.

Barcelona → Leading the way in waste management and smart lighting; a dense IoT network drastically reduced energy costs.

Dubai → AI traffic systems and block chain-powered services.

Atlanta (ranked #1 in the USA in 2025) has excellent connectivity and technological infrastructure.

Paris, the top city in Europe, consistently leads in mobility and sustainability metrics.

7. Prospects for the Future

6G, quantum-safe encryption, sophisticated digital twins, and AI-powered autonomous infrastructure will be the norm by 2030. Without relying on the cloud, edge AI will allow for millisecond decisions. The ultimate goal is an urban ecosystem that is genuinely human-centric, resilient, and sustainable—infrastructure that not only reacts to citizens' needs but also anticipates them.

The foundation of tomorrow's cities is smart technology, which is no longer a luxury. For the next century, urban life will be shaped by the systems we create today

Chapter 13

Engineering Solutions for Environment Challenges

Mr. Amit kumar Agarwal
Assistant professor dept of engineering madhav university sirohi

1. Introduction

Environmental concerns, such as climate change, water shortages, pollution, and resource depletion, are serious threats to the sustainability of the world's ecosystems and human societies. Engineering has a critical role to play in addressing these environmental challenges by utilizing the potential of innovation, technology, and sustainable design principles to reduce the impact of these environmental challenges. In this chapter, the various engineering approaches to these environmental challenges, including energy, water, waste, climate change, and infrastructure, will be examined. These approaches are informed by interdisciplinary knowledge from various fields of engineering, including mechanical, civil, chemical, and environmental engineering.

These environmental challenges are further compounded by the Intergovernmental Panel on Climate Change (IPCC), which has projected that by the mid-century, temperatures are likely to increase by 1.5 to 2 degrees Celsius in the absence of aggressive interventions to combat these environmental challenges. Engineering approaches to these environmental challenges are informed by the need to reduce the impact of these environmental challenges, as well as to adapt to the changes and impacts of these environmental challenges, such as resilient infrastructure. By 2026, advancements in AI, materials science, and biotech have accelerated these efforts, with investments in green technology exceeding $1.5 trillion globally each year. In this chapter, the various engineering approaches to these environmental challenges will be examined, including case studies and diagrams to ensure a comprehensive understanding of the concepts.

2. Renewable Energy Solutions for Climate Change Mitigation

The shift from fossil fuels to renewable energy is an important area of engineering in mitigating climate change. Engineers have developed various technologies to utilize renewable energy sources such as solar energy, wind energy, hydro energy, geothermal energy, and biomass energy. These technologies have been integrated into existing fossil fuel-based energy systems to ensure energy supply. Some of the innovations in renewable energy engineering include the development of high-efficiency photovoltaic panels that can generate up to 30% of the energy received from the sun. Another area of interest in solar energy engineering is the development of bifacial solar panels that can generate energy from both sides of the panels.

Engineers have also developed large blades for wind turbines that can reach 100 meters in length. These turbines can be installed on floating structures to generate energy in deep water. These turbines can generate up to 50% of the maximum available energy. The benefits of renewable energy engineering in mitigating climate change include the reduction of greenhouse gases that can be minimized by 70 to 80%. Renewable energy can also ensure energy security in various nations. For example, India has developed over 100 GW of solar energy capacity under the National Solar Mission by 2026. The country has also developed solar farms in Rajasthan that can function in desert environments.

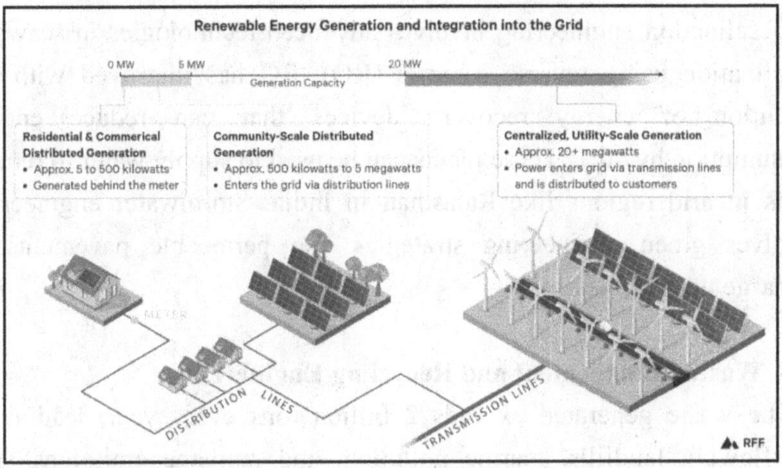

Figure: Integration of renewable energy sources into the power grid, illustrating scales from residential to utility-level generation.

3. Engineering Solutions for Water Resource Management

Water scarcity is currently affecting over 2 billion people worldwide. The problem is exacerbated by water pollution, overuse, and climate change. Engineering solutions to water resource management involve advanced water treatment processes, efficient distribution systems, and conservation strategies. Wastewater treatment plants utilize various water treatment processes to recycle water for reuse. This reduces water consumption by 30 to 50%.

The wastewater treatment process involves primary treatment in sedimentation tanks to remove suspended solids. The water is then transferred to secondary treatment tanks for biological treatment using an activated sludge system or membrane bioreactors. Finally, tertiary treatment involves water disinfection using UV light or ozonation. New technologies in wastewater treatment utilize forward osmosis and nanotechnology filters to increase water treatment efficiency. These filters can remove micro plastics and pharmaceuticals from wastewater with 99% efficacy.

Desalination engineering involves advanced technologies in seawater desalination using reverse osmosis (RO). RO has improved with the invention of energy recovery devices that can reduce energy consumption by 40%. These plants can be used to supply water to remote areas in arid regions like Rajasthan in India. Stormwater engineering involves green engineering strategies like permeable pavements to recharge water tables.

4. Waste Management and Recycling Engineering

The waste generated exceeds 2 billion tons every year, leading to overflowing landfills, marine pollution, and methane emissions. The engineering interventions aim to close the loop on the circular economy, reducing, reusing, and recycling waste. Advanced technologies employ AI-based optical sensors to sort waste with 95% accuracy, recycling 60-80% waste materials. The recycling process involves collecting waste, transporting it, sorting it manually or through advanced technologies, cleaning it, and finally processing it into raw materials. For plastic waste, chemical recycling through pyrolysis produces fuels or monomers to tackle non-recyclable plastic waste. Another engineering technique, bioremediation, uses microbes in landfills to decompose waste into raw materials, producing energy through the capture of biogas.

Electronic waste, or e-waste, recycling involves the hydrometallurgical process to obtain precious metals such as gold and copper, reducing the need for mining. For cities, the engineering technique uses decentralized composting plants to obtain fertilizer, reducing transportation emissions by 50%. Studies on waste reduction in Sweden show the implementation of near-zero waste engineering, recycling 99% waste materials.

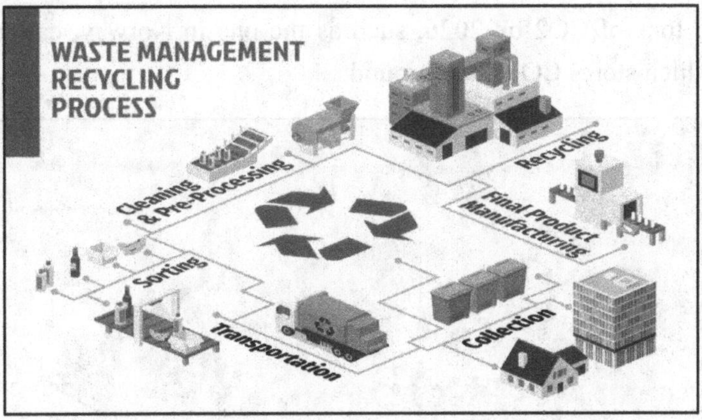

Figure: Diagram of the waste management and recycling cycle, highlighting collection, sorting, processing, and manufacturing stages.

5. Carbon Capture and Climate Mitigation Technologies

Engineering technologies to reduce the amount of carbon dioxide in the atmosphere are critical to mitigate the effects of global warming. Carbon capture technologies involve the capture, transport, and storage of CO2, or the use of captured CO2 to make products such as concrete.

The post-combustion capture technology uses solvents to capture CO2, which can be up to 90 percent efficient. Direct air capture technology, such as the one developed by Clime works, uses fans to capture CO2, which can be scaled up to capture one gigaton of CO2. Ocean-based technologies involve electrochemical carbon removal, where CO2 is absorbed by the oceans, and engineering alkalinity enhancement, where the oceans are made more alkaline to absorb more CO2.

Another technology is the bio energy with carbon capture, which combines biomass power plants with carbon capture technologies, which can result in negative emissions. These technologies are critical to the reduction of global warming, where it is expected to capture 10-20 gigatons of CO2 by 2050. Carbon capture technologies can capture 1.5

million tons of CO_2 by 2026, such as the one in Norway, called Long ship, which stores CO_2 underground.

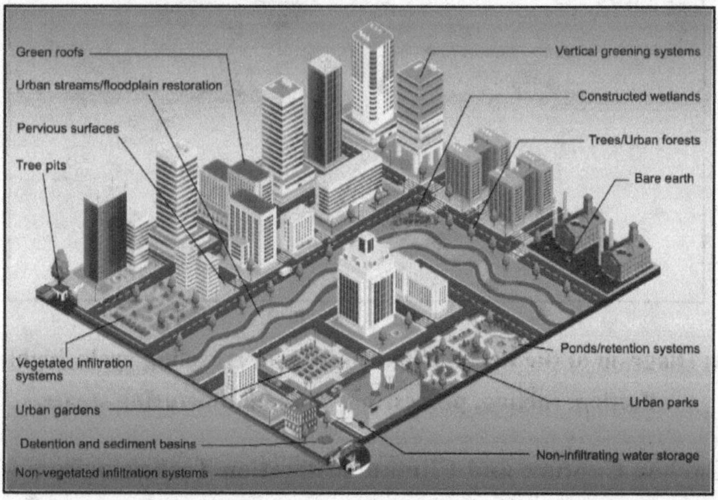

Figure: Diagram of green infrastructure elements in an urban setting, including green roofs, wetlands, and infiltration systems.

6. Challenges, Implementation Strategies, and Future Outlook

Though significant progress has been achieved, challenges remain to be overcome. These include high initial costs, technological scalability, policy hurdles, and community acceptability.

As we move forward to 2030 and beyond, new technologies will emerge. These include artificial intelligence-optimized technologies, nanotechnology for pollution management, and space-based solar power. These will be the breakthrough technologies of the future. The focus of engineers will be to create technologies that will be beneficial to the poorer communities of South Asia.

Conclusion

To conclude, the importance of engineering solutions for a more sustainable environment cannot be overstated. By engineering a healthier planet, we will be able to create a better world for the future.

MCQ Questions

1. Engineering innovation for social development mainly focuses on:

A. Profit maximization

B. Solving large-scale social problems

C. Increasing industrial output

D. Reducing labor cost

2. The concept of doing more with fewer resources is known as:

A. Smart engineering

B. Frugal engineering

C. Digital engineering

D. Industrial engineering

3. Jugaad innovation mainly promotes:

A. High-cost technology

B. Resourceful and flexible solutions

C. Traditional engineering methods

D. Automation only

4. Which technology is used to create customized prosthetic limbs at low cost?

A. Artificial Neural Network

B. 3D Printing

C. Blockchain

D. Laser cutting

5. The slow sand filter purifies water mainly through:

A. Chemical oxidation

B. Biological layer (Schmutzdecke)

C. UV radiation

D. Magnetic filtration

6. Solar-powered irrigation systems mainly use:

A. Diesel generators

B. Photovoltaic panels

C. Coal power

D. Steam turbines

7. Smart infrastructure integrates physical infrastructure with:

A. Manual monitoring

B. Digital technologies

C. Traditional systems

D. Mechanical devices only

8. In smart infrastructure architecture, sensors and actuators belong to:

A. Application layer

B. Network layer

C. Sensing layer

D. Data layer

9. Smart grids enable:

A. One-way electricity flow

B. Two-way communication of power and data

C. Only renewable energy generation

D. Manual power monitoring

10. Carbon capture technology helps to:

A. Increase fossil fuel usage

B. Reduce carbon dioxide in the atmosphere

C. Produce more greenhouse gases

D. Stop renewable energy production

Descriptive Questions

1. Explain the concept of engineering innovation for social development with examples.

2. Discuss the principles of engineering for social impact, including affordability, sustainability, and community participation.

3. Describe how frugal engineering helps improve healthcare access, particularly through low-cost prosthetics and diagnostics.

4. Explain the working principle and importance of frugal water purification systems such as slow sand filters.

5. Describe the role of solar-powered irrigation systems in improving agricultural productivity and sustainability.

6. Explain the concept and architecture of smart infrastructure systems.

7. Describe the layers of smart infrastructure architecture including sensing, network, data, and application layers.

8. Explain the working and benefits of smart grids in modern energy systems.

9. Discuss engineering solutions for water resource management, including wastewater treatment and desalination technologies.

10. Explain the importance of carbon capture technologies in climate change mitigation.

Chapter-14

Yoga as a Science of Holistic Health

Dr Niyanta
Assistant professor (Yoga), Department of physical education, Madhav university, Pindwara, Sirohi

Introduction

According to the WHO, health was defined in 1946.

"Health is a state of complete physical, mental and social well-being and not merely the absence of disease or infirmity".

In1986, the WHO made further clarifications:

"A resource for everyday life, not the objective of living. Health is a positive concept emphasizing social and personal resources, as well as physical capacities, state characterized by anatomic, physiologic, and psychological integrity; ability to perform personally valued family, work, and community roles; ability to deal with physical, biological, psychological, and social stress". According to Merriam Webster dictionary, "the condition of being sound in body, mind or spirit".

So, here it also gives the concept of mental and social health. Here, WHO indicate to the complete state of health.

Holistic comes from the Greek word "holos", which means complete or total. Holistic health includes complete or total health in which physical, mental, social and spiritual dimensions are included. By definition, holistic means "relating to or concerned with wholes or with complete systems rather than with the analysis of, treatment of, or dissection into parts."

The American Holistic Health Association (AHHA) presents health from a holistic perspective, emphasising that this ancient approach does not merely concentrate on illness or isolated body parts. Instead, it views the individual as a complete being and considers the dynamic interaction between a person and his or her environment. It highlights the integration of mind, body, and spirit, with the ultimate aim of achieving optimal well- being where all aspects of life function at their highest potential.

In contemporary discourse, health is generally understood through three major definitions. The first defines health as the absence of disease or physical impairment. The second view of health as a functional state that enables individuals to effectively manage the demands of everyday life, which also presumes freedom from illness. The third and more comprehensive definition describes health as a balanced state of equilibrium, one that exists both within the individual and in relation to the surrounding social and physical environment. In the modern era, however, there is a noticeable tendency to prioritise physical health while often neglecting mental, social, and spiritual dimensions. Yogic science addresses this imbalance by encompassing every layer of the human system, including the physical body, mental processes, emotional patterns, respiratory rhythms, and interpersonal relationships.

Yoga, as an ancient philosophy and practical system of well-being originated thousands of years ago. During its early development, human lifestyles were naturally active due to the demands of daily living. The absence of modern conveniences such as automobiles, household machines, and advanced infrastructure meant that physical exercise was inherently embedded in routine life. Therefore, Yoga did not emerge as a method to increase physical activity; rather, it evolved primarily as a system of healing with a profound emphasis on mental and inner well-being.

In contemporary society, Yoga is often narrowly identified with asanas (physical postures). However, asana represents only one component of a much broader therapeutic framework. In the *Yoga Sutras* of Patanjali, recognized asan authoritative classical text, only a small portion of the 195 sutras refers to asana practice. The majority elaborate on other transformative tools such as conscious breathing (pranayama), meditation, ethical lifestyle disciplines, dietary regulation, visualisation techniques, and the therapeutic use of sound. Collectively, these practices address the total human system: body, breath, mind and personality.

From the Ayurvedic perspective, health is conceptualized in an equally holistic manner. Ayurveda, traditionally regarded as an upaveda (subsidiary knowledge system) of the Vedas, developed an advanced framework of health care and medical science. It flourished historically in ancient centres of learning such as Nalanda, Takshashila, and Varanasi around 500–600 BCE and has experienced renewed global relevance following India's independence in 1947.

The renowned physician Maharshi Charaka defined health in classical Ayurvedic literature. Along with Vagbhata, he articulated the famous definition from the *Charaka Samhita*:

"Samadosha, samagnischasamadhatu mala kriyaha, Prasanna atmenindriya manaha swasthya ityabhidheeyate."
(CharakaSamhita15/41)

This definition explains that a healthy individual is one in whom the three doshas, vata, pitta, and kapha, remain in equilibrium; digestive fire (agni) functions optimally; bodily tissues (dhatus) and waste products (malas) operate normally; and the senses, mind, and soul exist in a state of contentment and harmony. Such a state is termed *swastha* (true health). Disease, conversely, represents a disturbance of this equilibrium. Thus, the holistic understanding of health has deep roots in ancient Indian knowledge traditions.

A similar multidimensional view is presented in the *Taittiriya Upanishad* through the Panchamaya Kosha model. The term *pancha*means "five," and *maya*denotes "pervasive layers." According to this model, human existence is not limited to the physical body alone; rather, it consists of five interconnected and interpenetrating sheaths or dimensions. These layers collectively illustrate the comprehensive and holistic nature of human health and consciousness.

Moving from the grossest to the most subtle level of human existence, the five dimensions of the individual may be understood as the physical body, breath, intellect, personality, and emotional sphere. This multidimensional view highlights that human beings cannot be fully understood or treated by focusing on only one aspect of their existence.

In contemporary medical science, the dominant model of health primarily emphasises physical, mental, and social well-being. While this framework has contributed significantly to disease management and life expectancy, it often gives limited attention to the spiritual dimension of health.

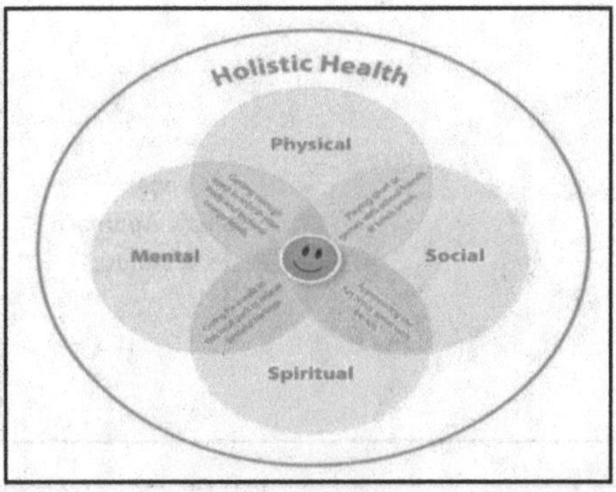

In contrast, Yoga and other ancient Indian knowledge systems adopt a more comprehensive perspective by including spiritual well-being as an essential component of health. Yogic philosophy maintains that many diseases originate from deeper imbalances within the inner self, and spiritual disharmonyis regarded as one of the fundamental root causes of suffering.

To illustrate this holistic framework, the analogy of a vehicle may be used. Just as a car requires all four wheels to function properly, human health rests upon four foundational pillars: physical, mental, social, and spiritual. The absence or weakness of anyone pillar results in imbalance, dissatisfaction, and adiminished quality of life. Thus, true well-being can only be achieved when all four dimensions are harmoniously developed.

Within the philosophical foundations of Yoga and Ayurveda, the concepts of *karma* and *samskara* are also considered significant in understanding disease causation. Deep-rooted impressions formed by past actions and experiences influence present behaviour, cognition, and health outcomes. Ignorance (*avidya*) or erroneous knowledge is viewed as a primary source of imbalance, leading to maladaptive lifestyles and psychosomatic disorders. Therefore, the removal of ignorance through right knowledge and self-realisation becomes a vital therapeutic process.

From this standpoint, spiritual health assumes the highest position among all dimensions of well-being, as it guides the individual toward liberation (*moksha*) and inner freedom. Consequently, both Yoga and Ayurveda place strong emphasis on not only the treatment of illness but also the preservation and promotion of health. Their primary objective is twofold: first, to maintain the well-being of a healthy individual, and second, to alleviate disease in those who are unwell.

Modern medical science, on the other hand, has historically focused more on disease prevention, diagnosis, and treatment. While preventive medicine is an important advancement, the ancient systems extend beyond prevention to emphasise sustained health maintenance, lifestyle harmony, and spiritual evolution as integral components of complete well-being.

Role of Yoga in Physical Health

Physical health refers to the extent to which an individual can realise aspirations, satisfy needs, adapt to environmental changes, and perform daily activities efficiently without physical disturbances. In this context, yoga plays a significant role in promoting and maintaining overall physical well-being.

According to Dr. Nevis, relaxation techniques incorporated in yoga practices help in alleviating chronic pain conditions such as lower back pain, arthritis, headaches, and carpal tunnel syndrome. Yoga has also been found to contribute to the reduction of high blood pressure levels.

Regular physical activity, including yogic practices, enhances muscular strength and endurance. Exercise facilitates the delivery of oxygen and nutrients to body tissues and improves the efficiency of the cardiovascular system. As heart and lung functions improve, individuals experience higher energy levels, enabling them to perform daily tasks more effectively.

Physical Benefits of Yoga

The regular practice of yoga offers numerous physical health benefits, including:

- Increased flexibility
- Enhanced muscle strength and tone
- Improved respiration, energy, and vitality
- Regulation of metabolism
- Weight management and reduction
- Better cardiovascular and circulatory health
- Improved athletic performance
- Protection from injuries

Scientific investigations have validated many of these benefits. Earlier studies established yoga's role in improving flexibility and muscular strength. More recent research confirms its positive impact on cardiovascular fitness, heart health, and lung capacity. Yoga is also considered an effective supportive tool for weight management. Active forms of yoga promote calorie expenditure, while gentler practices enhance body awareness, mindful eating, and lifestyle regulation, all of which contribute to healthy weight control.

Research Evidence Supporting Yoga for Physical Health

Several empirical studies highlight yoga's therapeutic value:

- **Santwana (2018)** reported that a 12-week intervention of yogasanaandpraṇayamaon40patientsresultedinasignificantreduction in fasting plasma glucose levels (*International Journal of Yoga*, 11(2), 129).
- **S. Dhananjai (2013)** conducted a study on 205 patients and found that 60 minutes of daily yoga practice significantly reduced psychological distress and waist circumference among obese women at the 0.001 level (*International Journal of Yoga*, 6(1), 66).
- **Jayram Gadham (2015)** examined the effects of yoga on obesity, hypertension, and lipid profile among 50 subjects. After three months of praṇayama and asana practice, a significant reduction in blood pressure was observed at the 0.01 level (*International Journal of Research in Medical Sciences*, 3, 1061–1065).

Role of Shat karmas in Physical Health

Shat karmas (six yogic cleansing techniques) purify the body and contribute to the preservation of health by preventing diseases. They function as preventive as well as therapeutic practices.

These cleansing processes are beneficial in managing and preventing disorders such as sinusitis, migraine, asthma, dust and pollen allergies, food allergies, halitosis, constipation, dysentery, kidney stones, skin diseases, acne, sexual dysfunction, insomnia, and anxiety disorders.

Shat karmas strengthen internal body systems, including:

- Digestive system
- Respiratory system
- Circulatory system
- Nervous system
- Immune system

By activating and balancing these vital systems, shat karmas promote holistic physical health.

Role of Asanas in Physical Health

Asanas constitute a fundamental component of yogic practice and play a significant role in the promotion of physical health. Their regular practice contributes to the development of muscular strength, endurance, and flexibility, while also enhancing joint mobility and postural stability. By facilitating efficient blood circulation, asanas ensure an adequate supply of oxygen and nutrients to body tissues, there by supporting optimal physiological functioning.

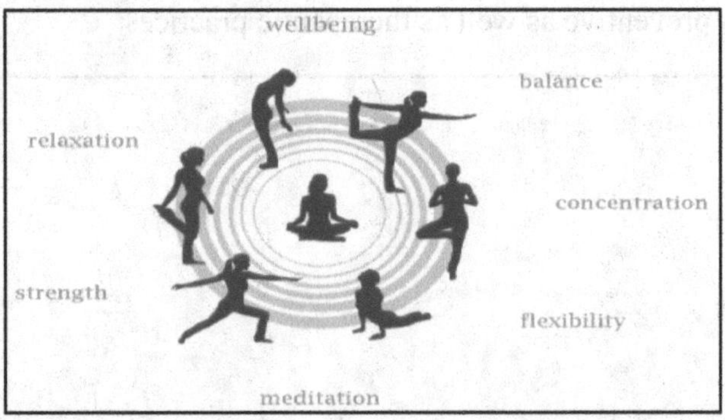

They exert beneficial effects on major body systems, including the cardiovascular, respiratory, digestive, and endocrine systems. Furthermore, the systematic stretching and relaxation involved in asana practice help alleviate fatigue, reduce musculoskeletal discomfort, and prevent various lifestyle related disorders. In addition, asanas assist in weight management, regulate metabolic processes and enhance overall physical vitality, enabling individuals to perform daily activities with greater efficiency and ease.

Role of Pranayama in Physical Health

Praṇayama, the yogic practice of controlled and regulated breathing, holds an important place in the promotion of physical health. It's regular practice improves the efficiency of the respiratory system by increasing lung capacity, strengthening the diaphragm and intercostal muscles, and facilitating optimal oxygen supply to body tissues. This enhanced oxygenation supports cellular functioning and over all vitality. Praṇayama like kapalbhati, bhastrika, and nadisuddhi, also exerts a positive effect on the cardio vascular system by helping to regulate heart rate, improve blood circulation, and assist in the management of blood pressure. In addition, it stimulates digestive and metabolic processes, thereby contributing to better assimilation of nutrients and elimination of toxins. By reducing physiological stress and balancing autonomic functions, praṇayama further supports immune competence. Therefore, through its multidimensional physiological effects, praṇayama serves as a valuable yogic tool for maintaining and enhancing physical health. Regular practice helps in preventing various physical ailments and contributes to the regulation of bodily doṣas, particularly Vata doṣa.

Role of Meditation in Physical Health

Meditation contributes to physical health by reducing cardiovascular strain. Chronic stress and hypertension force the heart to work harder, which may impair cardiac function over time.

Meditation, although traditionally regarded as a practice for mental and emotional refinement, has significant implications for physical health as well. Regular engagement in meditation, mindfulness and other practices contributes to the regulation of the autonomic nervous system, resulting in lowered heart rate, reduced blood pressure, and improved cardio vascular functioning. The state of deep relaxation achieved during meditation helps in decreasing the secretion of stress hormones, thereby promoting systemic physiological balance. Moreover, meditation supports immune functioning, enhances sleep quality, and assists in the management of chronic pain through its influence on neuro physiological mechanisms. By cultivating mindful awareness, it also encourages the adoption of healthier behavioral patterns that positively affect bodily health. Hence, meditation serves as an effective holistic intervention for the promotion and maintenance of physical well-being. Meditation helps lower cortisol (stress hormone) levels, thereby reducing the risk of stress-related disorders such as psychiatric illnesses, peptic ulcers, and migraines.

So, yoga is a comprehensive system that integrates physical postures, breathing techniques, cleansing processes, and meditation to promote optimal physical health. Supported by scientific evidence, yogic practices enhance strength, flexibility, cardio vascular efficiency, metabolic balance, and disease resistance, ultimately improving quality of life.

Role of Yoga in Mental Health

Mental health is an integral dimension of holistic well-being. It influences cognition, emotional balance, behaviour, and an individual's ability to cope with life situations. Yogic philosophy as well as modern scientific literature unanimously recosgnise yoga as a powerful tool for promoting mental health.

According to the World Health Organisation (WHO), "Mental heal this a state of well-being in which an individual realises his or her own abilities, can cope with the normal stresses of life, can work productively and can make a contribution to his or her community."

The WHO further stresses that mental health is not merely the absence of mental disorders, but also the presence of ongoing wellness, emotional resilience, and happiness.

Epidemiological evidence reported by the National Centre for Biotechnology Information (NCBI) indicates that the prevalence of psychiatricd is orders in India ranges from 9.5 to 370 per 1,000 population. Such variability is also reflected in international studies, highlighting the growing global burden of mental health problems and the need for integrative approaches such as yoga.

Yogic Scriptural Foundations of Mental Health

Ancient yogic texts extensively describe the relationship between the mind and health, emphasising that mastery over the mind is the key to psychological well-being.

Yoga vasiṣṭha

In the Yoga vasiatha, it is stated:

"Manah prasamana upaya yoga ityabhidhiyate."

(Nirvana Prakaraṇa, Uttarardha 13/3)

Yoga is the method of quieting the mind.

The scripture elaborates the concepts of Adhi (mental afflictions) and Vyadhi (physical diseases), explaining that many ailments originate in disturbed mental functioning. Thus, mental purification becomes essential for health.

Bhagavad Gita

In the Bhagavad Gita, Lord Krishna defines yoga as:

"samatvamyogauchyate." (2.48)

Equanimity of mind is called Yoga.

Mental balance in all situations is regarded as true yoga. This state of equipoise develops when one performs duties sincerely without attachment to outcomes, dedicateing results to the Divine. Such detachment reduces anxiety, stress and emotional turbulence.

Kathopanisad

The Katha Upanishad describes yoga as a state of innerst illness:

"Yada pancavatisthante jnanani manasa saha
Buddhis ca na vicestate tam ahuh paramam gatim.
Tam yogam iti manyante sthiram indriya dharanam."*(2.3.10–11)*

Whenever the senses and mind become pacified and the intellect ceases restless activity, the highest state of awareness is attained. This steady restraint of the senses is regarded as yoga. It requires vigilance and disciplined practice, as this state may arise and subside.

Patanjali Yoga Sutra

The Yoga Sutras of Patanjali provide the most systematic psychological framework of yoga.

"Yogas citta vrtti nirodhah"(1.2)

Yoga is the essation of the fluctuations of the mind.

The mind constantly engages in thinking, imagining, remembering, and doubting. These modifications (vṛttis) create restlessness. Yoga trains the practitioner to regulate and calm these patterns, leading to clarity, peace and self-realisation.

"dhyanaheyastadvrttayah" (2.11)

Meditation refines and dissolves deep mental patterns.

"sattva suddhih saumanasya ekagrya indriya jaya atmadarsana yogyatvani cha." (2.41)

Through purity (sauca) arise mental clarity, cheerfulness, concentration, sensory mastery, and readiness for self-realisation.

Other Yogic Texts

Gheraṇḍa Samhita states that pranayama, meditation, and Samadhi lead to mental equilibrium and liberation.

Amṛtabindu Upanisad declares:

"mana eva manusyanam karanam bandha moksayoh."

The mind alone is the cause of bondage and liberation. Attachment leads to suffering, while detachment leads to freedom.

Psycho physiological Impact of Yogic Practices

Yoga establishes harmony between mind and body, stabilising emotional and cognitive processes.

Kapalbhati

Kapalbhati is considered a frontal brain purification technique. It stimulates dormant neural centres, enhances subtle perception, and removes energetic blockages formed due to suppressed emotions. It is particularly useful in psychosomatic disorders characterised by negative thought patterns. It also exerts a soothing influence on the brain and is beneficial in conditions like migraine and epilepsy.

Vaman Dhauti & Shatkarmas

Vaman Dhauti facilitates the release of repressed emotions through physiological cleansing. Shat karmas influence the parasympathetic nervous system, inducing relaxation and autonomic balance.

Research by Megha Rastogi on female teachers demonstrated the positive psychosomatic impact of yogic cleansing practices.

Psychological Benefits of Regular Yoga Practice

Regulary of a practice enhances emotional regulation and self-mastery. As individuals gain control over bodily movements and breath, this control extends to thoughts and behaviour.

Key mental health benefits include:

- Reduced stress and anxiety
- Enhanced emotional stability
- Improved self-esteem and confidence
- Greater self-discipline
- Sense of inner control
- Relaxation and well-being

Yoga also serves as a natural physiological outlet for the fight-orflight stress response. Yogas an asstimulate the release of endorphins, the brain's natural tranquillisers, producing calmness and relaxation.

Research Evidence

Dr. Amanendra Mann (2019) conducted a 12-week study on 60 participants using a Happiness Questionnaire. The findings revealed a statistically significant increase in happiness levels (0.005 level) following regular shat karmas practice, demonstrating yoga's positive psychological effects. A study conducted by Shohani et al. (2018) found that following four weeks of regular Haṭha Yoga practice, the researchers observed a statisticallysignificantanxietyreduction($p<0.0001$),stress($p<0.0001$), and depression ($p < 0.001$) levels, indicating the effectiveness of short-termyogicinterventioninimprovingpsychologicalwell-being.Similarly, Singphow et al. (2022) found that after sixteen weeks of structured yoga intervention, participants demonstrated significant reductions in stress, anxiety, and depression. In addition to psychological improvements, notable enhancements were recorded in spinal mobility, including spinal flexion ($p <0.001$), spinal extension($p< 0.001$), right lateral flexion($p = 0.001$),and left lateral flexion ($p =0.007$) among eighty participants with chronic low back pain. Furthermore, Turmel et al. (2022) concluded that after fourteen weeks of daily Vini yoga practice, significant improvements were observed in sleep quality ($p<0.001$). Additionally, reductions were noted in anxiety ($p < 0.05$), depression ($p < 0.001$), daytime sleepiness ($p <0.05$), fatigue ($p<0.01$), and the number of nocturnal arousals($p<0.01$) in a single-group pre–post study involving twenty-one participants.

So, both classical yogic scriptures and contemporary scientific research affirm yoga's profound role in mental health promotion. By quieting mental fluctuations, cultivating emotional balance, regulating neuro physiological responses, and fostering self-awareness, yoga serves as a holistic and preventive approach to psychological well-being. In the modern era of escalating mental stress, yoga offers a time-tested, integrative, and sustainable pathway to mental harmony.

Role of Yoga in Social Health

"Social health constitutes an essential dimension of holistic well-being, reflecting an individual's capacity to establish meaningful relationships and function effectively within society." According to the World Health Organisation (WHO):

"Social health can be defined as our ability to interact and form meaningful relationships with others. It also relates to how comfortably we can adapt in social situations. Social relationships have an impact on our mental health, physical health, and mortality risk."

Thus, social health encompasses the ability to develop satisfying interpersonal relationships, adapt comfortably to diverse social environments, and behave appropriately across different settings.

Yoga and Enhancement of Social Well-Being

Yoga contributes significantly to social health by fostering emotional balance, positive attitudes, and harmonious behaviour. The integration of body and mind through yogic practices enhances mood and emotional stability. A healthy body supports a healthy mind, which in turn promotes constructive social interaction.

Regular practice of asana and praṇayama stimulates the production of neurotransmitters such as endorphins, which generate positive feelings, reduce irritability and encourage prosocial behaviour. Yoga not only improves physical flexibility but also cultivates psychological flexibility, enabling individuals to respond more patiently and empathetically in social contexts.

Yama: The Social Ethics of Yoga

Within the framework of Aṣṭanga Yoga, the first limb, Yama, directly addresses social health. Yamas are ethical restraints that regulate interpersonal conduct and promote social harmony. Maharshi Patanjali enumerates five yamas in the Yoga Sutras of Patanjali (2.30):

"ahimsa satya asteya brahmacarya aparigrahah yamaḥ."

The Five Yam as and Their Social Significance

1. **Ahimsa (Non-violence):** The principle of non-harm in thought, word, and action. It fosters compassion, tolerance, and peaceful coexistence.
2. **Satya (Truthfulness):** Encourages honesty and integrity in communication and behaviour, strengthening trust in relationships.
3. **Asteya (Non-stealing):** Promotes respect for others' rights and property, reducing exploitation and social conflict.
4. **Brahmacharya (Self-restraint):** Implies moderation and responsible conduct, contributing to moral and relational stability.
5. **Aparigraha (Non-possessiveness):** Cultivates freedom from greed and excessive attachment, encouraging simplicity and social

equity. Collectively, these ethical principles nurture patience, mutual respect, and responsible social living.

Emotional Refinement and Social Harmony

Patañjali further outlines attitudes essential for emotional and social well-being:

"maître karuna mudita upeksanam sukha duhkha punyapuṇya visayanam bhavanatascitta prasadanam." (Yoga Sutra 1.33)

The mind becomes purified by cultivating:

- **Friendliness (Maitri)** toward the happy
- **Compassion (Karuṇa)** toward the suffering
- **Joy (Mudita)** toward the virtuous
- **Equanimity (Upeksa)** toward the non-virtuous

These attitudes foster emotional maturity, reduce jealousy and hostility, and promote harmonious social relationships.

Social Values in the Bhagavad Gita

The Bhagavad Gita also highlights virtues essential for social health.

Qualities of an Ideal Devotee

"abhayam sattvasanshuddhir jnanayogavyavasthitih
danaṁ damash cha yajnash cha svadhyayas tapa arjavam
ahinsa satyam akrodhas tyagah shantir apaishunam
daya bhuteshv aloluptvam mardavam hrir achapalam
tejah kshama dhritih śhaucham adroho natimanita
bhavanti sampadaṁ daivim abhijatasya bharata" \\ (16\1,2,3)
Bhagwad Geeta

Lord Krishna describes an ideal individual as one who is free from malice, friendly, compassionate, egoless, forgiving, and balanced in happiness and sorrow. Such a person has self-controlled, content, and dedicated qualities that strengthen social cohesion.

Divine Social Virtues (16.1–3)

In Chapter16, Krishna enumerates divine qualities conducive to righteous social living, including:

- Fearlessness
- Purity of mind
- Charity
- Self-control
- Non-violence
- Truthfulness
- Absence of anger
- Compassion for all beings
- Gentleness and modesty
- Forgiveness and fortitude
- Cleanliness and absence of hatred

These virtues collectively form the ethical foundation of a healthy and progressive society.

So, Yoga serves as a comprehensive system for nurturing social health by integrating ethical discipline, emotional refinement, and psychological balance. Through the practice of yamas, cultivation of positive attitudes, and embodiment of scriptural virtues, individuals develop compassion, cooperation, and social responsibility. In contemporary society, where interpersonal stress and social fragmentation are increasing, yoga offers a timeless pathway toward harmonious social living and collective well- being.

Role of Yoga in Spiritual Health

Spiritual health represents the highest dimension of holistic well-being. It reflects an individual's search for deeper meaning, purpose, and connection with the self, others, nature, and the Supreme Reality. When a person is spiritually healthy, life decisions become clearer, actions align with inner values, and one experiences harmony, fulfilment, and inner peace.

Spiritual wellness nurtures qualities such as compassion, love, forgiveness, altruism, joy, and contentment. Religious faith, moral values, beliefs, and ethical principles often shape spirituality and help individuals realise their highest potential.

Yoga as the Path to Spiritual Liberation

Yoga is traditionally regarded as a path of liberation(*mokṣa*). It guides the practitioner from illusion (*avidya*) to ultimate reality (*satya*). Although yoga is not confined to any single religion, its practices are deeply spiritual innature. Yogic disciplines cultivate inner awareness, self-transformation, and union with the higher consciousness.

The Sanskrit root **"Yuj"**, from which the term yoga is derived, means *to unite* or *toyoke*. It signifies the union of the individuals elfm (*jivatman*) with the universal self (*paramatman*). This pursuit of union forms the philosophical foundation of yoga's spiritual dimension.

Through meditation, pranayama, and introspective practices, individuals beg into witness their own breath, thoughts, and life processes. This witnessing attitude reduces attachment and karmic bondage, ultimately leading toward liberation.

Spiritual Discipline in Patanjali Yoga

The Yoga Sutras of Patanjali provide a systematic framework for spiritual evolution.

Practice and Detachment

"abhyasa vairagyabhyam tan nirodhaḥ"(1.12)

Mental modifications are restrained through sustained practice (*abhyasa*) and detachment (*vairagya*). These two pillars gradually purify consciousness and prepare the aspirant for higher spiritual realisation.

Niyama: Observances for Spiritual Health

In Aṣṭanga Yoga, **Niyama** represents personal observances that cultivate inner discipline and spiritual growth:

"sasuca santoṣa tapaḥ svadhyaya Isvara praṇidhanani niyamaḥ." (2.32)

1. **Sauca (Purity):** External cleanliness and internal purification of the mind.
2. **Santosa (Contentment):** Acceptance and satisfaction with what one has.
3. **Tapas (Austerity):** Disciplined effort and spiritual perseverance.
4. **Svadhyaya (Self-study):** Study of the self and sacred scriptures.
5. **Isvara Pranidhana (SurrendertotheDivine):** Devotional surrender and trust in higher consciousness.

These observances refine character and orient the practitioner toward spiritual awareness.

Kaivalya: The State of Liberation

Patanjali describes the ultimate spiritual goal:

"puruṣaartha sunyanam gunanam pratiprasavah kaivalyam svarupapratistha va citisaktihriti||" (4\34) patanjali yoga sutra

Liberation (*kaivalya*) occurs when the three guṇas, sattva, rajas, and tamas, recede to their source, and pure consciousness abides in its own true nature. This state corresponds to self-realisation beyond mental conditioning.

Spiritual Wisdom in the Bhagavad Gita

The Bhagavad Gita elaborates spiritual health through the concept of *sthitaprajna,* one established indivine wisdom.

Transcendence of Desires

"prajahati yada kaman sarvan partha manogatan
atmanevatmana tuṣhṭaḥ sthitaprajnas tadochyate"(2\55) Bhagwad *Geeta*

A spiritually evolved person abandons selfish desires and remains content in the Self.

Control of the Senses

"yada sanharate chayam kurmo nganiva sarvashaḥ
indriyanindriyarthebhyas tasya prajn apratishthita"\\ (1\58)
Bhagwad Geeta

One who withdraws the senses like a tortoise withdrawing its limbs is firmly established in wisdom.

Inner Awakening

"ynisha sarvabhutanam tasyam jagarti sanyami
yasyaṁjagrati bhatani sa nisha pashyato muneh"\\ (2\69)
Bhagwad *Geeta*

What appears as darkness to the worldly is awakening for the spiritually aware.

Freedom from Ego and Desire

"vihaya Kaman yaḥ sarvan pumansh charati nihsprihaḥ
Nirmamo nirahankaraḥ sa shantim adhigachchhati"// (2\71)
Bhagwad *Geeta*

Abandoning desires, ego, and possessiveness leads to perfect peace.

Self-Satisfaction

"yas tvatmaratir eva syad atmatṛiptash cha manavaḥ
Atmanyeva cha santuṣhṭas tasya karyaṁ na vidyate"\\(3\17)
Bhagwad *Geeta*

One who rejoices in the Self alone transcends worldly obligations.

Brahmic State

"eṣha brahmi sthitiḥ partha nainam prapya vimuhyati
Sthitvasyam antakale pi brahmanirvanam richchhati"//(2/72)
Bhagwad Geeta

Established in this enlightened state, one is freed from delusion and attains liberation from the cycle of birth and death.

Spiritual Transformation Through Yogic Practice

Yoga's spiritual dimension lies in its capacity to transform consciousness. It develops intuitive wisdom, ethical sensitivity, and universal compassion. By practising meditation and breath awareness, individuals cultivate detachment, witness consciousness, and karmic freedom. A spiritually awakened person turns in ward, seeking truth within rather than in external possessions. Gradually, unnecessary desires diminish, leading to lasting peace and self-realisation.

So, yoga offers a comprehensive pathway to spiritual health by integrating disciplined practice, ethical living, self-study, devotion, and meditative absorption. Rooted in classical scriptures and experiential wisdom, yoga guides the practitioner from restlessness to stillness, from ignorance to knowledge, and ultimately from bondage to liberation (*mokṣa*). In this way, yoga fulfils the highest purpose of human existence realisation of one's true spiritual nature.

Conclusion

Yoga presents a comprehensive framework for understanding and achieving holistic health. It teaches that true well-being is not limited to the absence of disease but encompasses the harmonious integration of physical, mental, social, and spiritual dimensions of human life. For the attainment and maintenance of optimal health, it is essential to cultivate balance across all these domains. In contrast to modern medical science, which has traditionally focused primarily on physical and mental health, yoga adopts a multidimensional approach. It recognises that human existence operates simultaneously at gross and subtle levels; therefore, well-being must also bead dressed at social and spiritual planes. A life that is physically fit and mentally sound but socially disconnected or spiritually unfulfilled remains in complete.

Yoga further emphasises that the ultimate aim of human life extends beyond health toward self-realisation and liberation (mokṣa).Holistic perfection across all aspects of living prepares the aspirant for this higher spiritual pursuit. From a practical perspective, yogic techniques influence both the gross physical body and the subtle energy body (praṇamayakosa). Asanas do not merely enhance muscular strength and flexibility; they also regulate praṇic flow and stimulate psycho-energetic centres (chakras). For instance, back-bending postures are traditionally associated with activation of the heart chakra (anahata), which is linked with emotional qualities such as love, compassion, empathy, and freedom from jealousy or egoism. Similarly, praṇayama, mudra, and bandha practices exert multidimensional effects, physiological, psychological, and energetic. They enhance vital energy (praṇa), stabilise mental processes, and purify subtle channels (naḍis). Meditation further deepens this process by promoting neurochemical balance, enhancing positive neurotransmitter activity, calming emotional reactivity, and cultivating inner peace. It reduces excessive attachment as well as aversion, thereby supporting spiritual equilibrium.

Different streams of yoga collectively contribute to holistic development. Systems such as Aṣṭanga Yoga, Niṣkama Karma Yoga, Mantra Yoga, Japa Yoga, Laya Yoga, Nada Yoga, Bhakti Yoga, Jnana Yoga, Haṭha Yoga, and Raja Yogaaddress diverse aspects of human personality. While some emphasise action, others devotion, knowledge, sound, or meditative absorption, yet all converge toward integrated health and spiritual awakening.

Thus, yoga serves as a transformative science that leads individuals from imbalance to harmony, from restlessness to tranquillity and ultimately from bondage to freedom. By nurturing physical vitality, mental clarity, social harmony, and spiritual awareness, yoga guides humanity toward the ultimate goal of life, truth, peace and the ultimate goal liberation.

Answer the Multiple Choice Questions

1. According to the World Health Organization (1946), health is defined as:

A. Absence of disease

B. Physical fitness only

C. Complete physical, mental and social well-being

D. Spiritual enlightenment

2. The term "Holistic" is derived from the Greekword:

A. Som

B. Holos

C. Logos

D. Ethos

3. Who defined heal thin the Charaka Samhitaas "Samadosha, samagnischa…"?

A. Vagbhata

B. Sushruta

C. Charaka

D. Patanjali

4. The Panchamaya Kosha concept is described in which Upanishad?

A. Katha Upanishad

B. Taittiriya Upanishad

C. Mundaka Upanishad

D. Isha Upanishad

5. "Yogas chitta vritti nirodhah" is mentioned in:

A. Bhagavad Gita

B. Hatha Yoga Pradipika

C. Yoga Sutras of Patanjali

D. Gheranda Samhita

6. Which of the following is not a Yama?

A. Ahimsa

B. Satya

C. Saucha

D. Aparigraha

7. According to the Bhagavad Gita, "Samatvam yoga uchyate" means:

A. Yoga is meditation

B. Yoga is detachment

C. Equanimity is yoga

D. Yoga is union

8. Which shatkriya is particularly useful in managing sinusitis and respiratory disorders?

A. Trataka

B. Nauli

C. Neti

D. Kapalbhati

9. Pranayama primarily improves:

A. Digestive enzymes only

B. Respiratory efficiency and autonomic balance

C. Bone density

D. Vision

10. The ultimate goal of Yoga according to Patanjali is:

A. Physical fitness

B. Mental relaxation

C. Kaivalya (Liberation)

D. Social harmony

Give the answer of these questions in a descriptive manner.

1. Explain the concept of holistic health according to the World Health Organization and yogic philosophy.

2. Describe the Ayurvedic definition of health given by Charaka and explain its components.

3. Discuss the Panchamaya Kosha model and its relevance to holistic health.

4. Explain the role of Yoga in promoting physical health with suitable research evidence.

5. Describe the importance of Shatkarmas in maintaining physical health.

6. Discuss the psychological benefits of Yoga with reference to classical yogic texts.

7. Explain the concept of Yama and its contribution to social health.

8. Describe how meditation contributes to both physical and mental well-being.

9. Explain the spiritual dimension of health with reference to the Bhagavad Gita.

10. Discuss the ultimate aim of Yoga and explain the concept of Kaivalya.